ref

A Systemic Treatment of Bulimia Nervosa

Inside Anorexia
Bringing together the Stories of Sufferers and their Families
Christine Halse, Anne Honey and Desiree Boughtwood
ISBN 978 1 84310 597 8

Drawing from Within
Using Art to Treat Eating Disorders
Lisa D. Hinz
ISBN 978 1 84310 822 1

Bulimia Nervosa
A Cognitive Therapy Programme for Clients
Myra Cooper, Gillian Todd and Adrian Wells
ISBN 978 1 85302 717 8

In and Out of Anorexia
The Story of the Client, the Therapist and the Process of Recovery
Tammie Ronen and Ayelet
ISBN 978 1 85302 990 5

Arts Therapies and Clients with Eating Disorders
Fragile Board
Edited by Ditty Dokter
ISBN 978 1 85302 256 2

Anorexics on Anorexia
Edited by Rosemary Shelley
ISBN 978 1 85302 471 9

Self-Mutilation and Art Therapy
Violent Creation
Diana Milia
ISBN 978 1 85302 683 6

More Than Just a Meal
The Art of Eating Disorders
Susan R. Makin
Foreword by Bryan Lask
ISBN 978 1 85302 805 2

A Systemic Treatment of Bulimia Nervosa

Women in Transition

Carole Kayrooz

Foreword by a service user

Jessica Kingsley Publishers
London and Philadelphia

First published in the United Kingdom in 2001
by Jessica Kingsley Publishers
116 Pentonville Road
London N1 9JB, UK
and
400 Market Street, Suite 400
Philadelphia, PA 19106, USA

www.jkp.com

Copyright © Carole Kayrooz 2001
Printed digitally since 2007

Library of Congress Cataloging in Publication Data
A CIP catalogue record for this book is available from the Library of Congress

British Library Cataloguing in Publication Data
A CIP catalogue record for this book is available from the British Library

ISBN 978 1 85302 918 9

Contents

Acknowledgements

There are many people I would like to thank for their contribution to the conception and development of this book. First and foremost, thanks should go to the women who have been my clients, from whom I learnt so much. In particular, thanks to the three women who gave so generously by agreeing for me to include their case studies, based on their actual therapy sessions. One other special young woman agreed to write her own version of her experience in therapy. This is included as the Foreword of this book. She said that she found writing this a useful activity, and it was such a useful process for both of us that I now wonder if such an exercise would be a good way for others to bring to closure the relationship and the experience.

There have been many contributors to the conceptual framework of this book. Acknowledgement is made throughout the text but mention should be made here of the works of Gregory Bateson and the writings and workshops of many within the systemic therapy network, notably Michael White, Mara Selvini-Palazzoli, Boscolo, de-Shazer and Watzlawick. Others have offered clinical assistance along the way, Adelle Hamilton and Gayelene Clews for their clinical advice and collaboration.

Very special thanks should go to Jerry Olsen and Professor Tony Shaddock for their academic support and friendship throughout the Masters thesis that was the impetus of the book and their sponsorship of the development of the manuscript itself. Many thanks should also go to my students, too numerous to mention, who, over the past six years, have continued to prompt me to be rigorous in my exploration of the topic.

Finally, I have my partner Robert to thank for his checking of the manuscript and Amy Lankester-Owen of Jessica Kingsley Publishers for her editing. Others have helped along the way too, namely JoAnn

McGreevy and Dr Charles Price. I am grateful to all these people for assisting me to bring the book to fruition.

Special Note

Preliminary versions of some sections in Chapters Two and Seven were originally published in the *Australian and New Zealand Journal of Family Therapy*, the *Dulwich Centre Newsletter* and *The Australian Counselling Psychologist*. They appear here in substantially revised and enlarged form.

Preface

I once had a friend who studied painting at a large art school. Her paintings were small pearls in a then popular expressionistic sea. Others in her studio were splashing muddied paint on to huge canvases, while she tended to precise strokes on modest and luminescent works. Her painting intrigued me and I wanted to know more. I asked her to lunch. Her ambivalence about our proposed meeting was confusing. She said she could come, then she said she could not. Then, after we arranged an alternative time, she backed down at the last moment.

After several of these sorts of episodes, I finally met her at a café. She seemed her usual self, troubled but with a child-like readiness for fun, her big hands pulling back her sleeves. At a break in our conversation, she leaned across the table and said she could not come to a proposed dinner to meet my family. Then she took a long silence. In the conversation that followed, she said she was embarrassed to tell me that she was a member of Overeaters Anonymous and that she had to go to one of their meetings instead of coming to dinner. She said she was bulimic and would eat until she vomited.

She described to me in detail the kind of lifestyle the disorder created for her – the secrecy and aloneness, the self-disgust provoked by the ritualistic behaviour and the obsession with weight and food that punctuated her days. Although eventually I lost touch with her as a friend, I never lost the profound sense of recognition of certain themes in the conversation that related to the experience of other women. It seemed as though women suffering from bulimia nervosa were not a discrete pathological group but one existing on the extreme end of a continuum shared by many, possibly the majority, of other women. This book is dedicated not only to those women who have experienced bulimia nervosa but to all women who have experienced a disordered relationship with food. It is especially dedicated to our daughters.

Foreword

by a service user

As a young girl at high school I was a typical high achiever (school captain and so on). I strived to achieve in academia, sport, school theatre and school councils. I mostly did this as a way of gaining my mother's and the broader world's approval. I remember during this time that my mother's boyfriend started taunting me about my weight. He referred to me as the elephant and said he needed to hide food if I was around. I was slightly heavy but, looking back, I realise there was no way I was 'fat'. However, during school years 10 and 11 (aged 15 and 16) I became fanatical about losing weight and began to learn about the calorie value of every item I ate. I became very disciplined about what I ate and as I trimmed off I received flattering compliments and my mother's boyfriend was silenced.

During my final year of school I was very focused upon my studies and consciously decided not to worry about food, as I wanted to focus 100 per cent on achieving a high academic result. I thought this would mean I would gain weight but accepted this, knowing I could address the problem another year. Interestingly enough, as I threw myself into studies and the general school life and forgot about food I actually lost weight.

On completion of high school, I achieved a place in medicine at a large university. However, mainly due to my mother's concerns about paying university fees and my interest in the outdoors, sport and adventure, I decided instead to join the military. Here I would undertake intensive study at university. On arrival at the military establishment, I was placed into a unit of 40 other trainees that were predominantly male. I soon received a variety of pep talks about girls and their weight. I remember one senior male trainee telling me that I had a nice figure now but needed to be very careful as the majority of the girls lost it within six months in the military. I soon learnt that slim, fit, celibate girls were accepted; others were not.

Females in the military appeared to be discussed in great detail by the male trainees. In the common room as a first year trainee, I would be vacuuming the floor or cleaning the kitchen area quietly listening to endless stories of which girls had put on weight, speculation on their sexual lives and stories of girls failing to achieve. All of this was 'evidence' that girls did not belong and could not do the job as well as male trainees. Every mistake a female made was discussed in great detail with accompanying slanderous remarks.

I was desperate to be accepted and to fit in and terrified of being one of the girls who was regularly discussed in public. I made it a golden rule not to sleep with anyone and spent much time training and watching my weight. The males in my division were friendly on a one-on-one basis and saw you as a sister or someone to protect, but possibly never as an equal. On going to meals, if you ever got dessert all the guys would create a commotion with loud exclamations in the communal food hall. They'd yell, 'You'll get fat!', 'Ohhhh…. She's started going for desserts' and so on.

'Piggy' was a term used to describe anyone who was lazy, fat and could not keep up in physical training. Conversely it was also a word used to describe all females. Guys would talk to you in a friendly manner, 'How are you going, Piggy?'. 'Piggy' was a term used to describe a fat 'arse' or a piggy's arse. Guys would constantly talk about the size of girls' 'piggies' as a hobby. At other times, while in the military, females were hated with such intensity that it was fearful, like seeing group hysteria. I remember a girlfriend and I clutched each other as we talked about it and started crying.

Females did not get together much and in my unit I was the only girl in my year so I tended to hang around with the guys all the time.

On reflection I now see how the females became very withdrawn. We all wore non-sexual, sensible clothes and feminism was a word that was never mentioned. Females getting together and talk of female issues was offensive to the male culture and so it did not happen much.

In my first year in the military, I was so scared of developing a 'piggy' that I was immensely disciplined and strict with my eating. I lost a lot of weight and got down to being the skinniest I'd ever been. When I returned home for Easter break my sister and family admired me for what I'd become. I lost the sense of eating when I was hungry and ignored my body's messages. Eating was a constant issue in my mind; I was obsessed with calculating calories and training.

After a while I started to binge eat. I found I'd suddenly turn into an unthinking animal that just could not stop eating. Bingeing meant you'd go into this panic-frenzied state where the voice that was constantly calculating calories would be firmly squashed by an instinctive drive. You'd rush from one take-away outlet to the next, eating on the way. You couldn't stand your mouth not having food in it. You could only stop when you felt so sick you could hardly walk. Vomiting became a necessity to relieve the pain in the stomach and it also relieved some of the guilt you felt for over-eating. Once the 'crazy' phase had passed there was a phase of immense guilt and self-reproach; I would calculate what needed to be done to repair the damage and plan a strict week ahead to punish myself. Once I went for three days without any food.

These bouts of bingeing (usually on a weekend) followed by a strict week of dieting and exercise became almost the norm and I started to put on weight. Comments were made as guys would come and confidentially tell me, 'Did you know you're starting to put on weight?' Senior girls would call me up in front of the group and stick their fingers inside my skirt waistband to feel how tight it was. At various times during this period I felt immensely depressed and suicidal. I did not want to be in this world but knew that I couldn't put my family through the trauma of my death. This made me feel trapped. I had no girlfriends, no hobbies or interests. I simply lived trying to win the battle for acceptance through trying to control my body. I went to see a civilian doctor who prescribed me anti-depressants. I didn't tell him about the bulimia. I took these for two days then told a male friend and we threw them in the bin. I hated the idea that I was taking drugs. The doctor offered no counselling or talking; it was simply, just take these.

I went to the civilian doctor because I didn't want anyone in the military knowing about my condition. In the end it was all too tortuous and I knew I needed help. I made an appointment with the military female doctor and blurted everything out. I could not stop crying and could hardly speak. I remember a student doctor was in the room as well, and seeing the horrified expression on her face. The military doctor assured me of privacy and arranged for me to see a civilian lady psychologist, Carole Kayrooz. It was terrifying to come forward and I was also nerve-wracked to see Carole. I hated the idea that I wasn't in control or would be seen as some sort of disgusting freak.

Carole put me at ease straight away and speaking with her was such a great outlet from that weird military world. I cannot remember all the specifics of the treatment, but overall it was an impression of bringing my thinking back to normal. It all seemed soothing and helped to gradually reduce my panic states. The areas I remember which were most helpful were: identifying and questioning irrational thoughts: specifically, the idea that fat = bad, lazy, weak; and looking at what bulimia was doing to me.

Carole went through the physiological aspects and I was horrified about the effects this could have on my heart and health. Carole asked me to visualise life without bulimia and asked where I'd like to go in my life. We talked about what life could be like without bulimia. I came to think about all the emotional, intellectual and physical time bulimia took from my life. A future of being free of bulimia was about being happy and relaxed and finding time for hobbies and other interests. We spent a while weighing up the pros and cons of continuing as a bulimic or of breaking away from it. I came to really want to break away from it but breaking the pattern was a lot harder than talking about it. It was distressing to know how bad it was and still to keep falling into binges.

From the start Carole gave me two goals or rules: at all costs, eat three well-balanced meals a day, (even if I'd binged I had to do this; no more vomiting.

From accepting these two rules I knew my two 'outs' were gone and that I would have to accept putting on weight. However, I was prepared to suffer weight gain to break the cycle. Short-term pain and humiliation in the military was worth freeing myself for life from bulimia. Carole talked about the worst case scenario of putting on weight. She said if I did, was that the end of the world? Was I still a good person? Did I know people who were 'chubby' and still think that they were good people? Fat is not a big deal, who cares? So what; 'Like it or lump it' was the attitude I'd need to have with the guys.

This period of not vomiting and eating three meals was hard. Still I continued to binge and couldn't break out of it. I felt as though I'd failed Carole. It was as though my body was determined to make up for the years of diets or was preparing itself for the next round of dieting. I deprived myself so long of sweets that I still kicked into that panicked, frenzied unthinking phase where I couldn't stop myself.

It was hard to break this cycle. Carole gave me some other activities to do. These were:

1. Allowing myself one 'bad' food item a day. Through allowing myself a chocolate bar a day I came to see 'bad' foods as less forbidden.

2. Eating bad food in public. This involved eating a chocolate bar in the common room, which was a massive act of defiance and drew many comments. It was hard, but allowed me to stop having this 'hidden' life and to show that I was not denying myself all the time.

3. Planning a binge and sitting down and eating it all. The first activity of a planned binge filled me with revulsion and it was

awful to sit and eat everything. I guess it allowed me to eat a large quantity while not in the 'panicked' state. It made me see how awful it was.

4. There was a rule that if I binged I would have to eat exactly the same food the next day. This was similar to the above, in that while in the midst of the 'panic' it helped me to break out of that 'panic' state. While bingeing I'd suddenly realise that I had to do this tomorrow. I guess that triggered a message to my instincts, 'Relax, you'll be getting heaps of food tomorrow too so you don't need to stock up for a fasting period'. It was like a more extreme version of the three meals a day rule.

5. A task was to write down each night the good things I had done for the day. These were things which were 'good' in terms of looking after myself: for example, allowing myself some recreational, relaxation activity; doing sport; participating in a social activity; standing up for myself against the guys. I found this activity had a powerful effect. First it started me thinking about other things in life and my mental and emotional energy became redirected away from food. Also it helped me to start thinking about meeting my needs, which had a terrific impact on my self-esteem. I realise that the military culture, and the way I lived in it, was greatly about the denial of my needs and the suppression of my personality and femininity. Carole suggested bulimia was positive part of me 'rebelling' against this culture and refusing to be denied. She asked me in what other ways I could rebel, and this was about being my own person despite the culture. Succeeding in the military was a form of rebellion as well. Relieving myself of bulimia would allow me more time to focus on achieving highly.

By the time I'd reached third year I came to see the culture for what it was: just some stupid immature young boys attempting to underline their superiority through destroying anything that was 'other' than them. In first year I had believed and lived what the 'culture' had said and now I could see it as crap. I also started to meet more girls in my year and this was a relief, to talk to them about the idiot blokes. It made you realise that it hadn't just been you, it was the place.

It took me about two to three years totally to rid myself of bingeing. Over those years I became sickened by thinking about food and tended to focus on the three meals thing, and then if I had a minor binge I ignored it as an irritating after-effect.

I had a short relapse a couple of years later when I found myself again in a strange male culture. Here the males were all competing to sleep with me and a number of them lied and tricked me. Here I felt I became the other thing I had most feared in the military, 'a loose woman'. This was traumatic as well. I applied the same rationale to my situation. Throughout my university years I had denied myself my sexuality and had acted out the 'pure Angel' role required of me. A backlash was possibly to be expected and was possibly a healthy sign. On reflection, I had not slept around very much at all but the culture labelled me as bad. I decided that this assessment of me as a 'loose woman' was wrong. So through that reassessment, I learnt to be more in tune with my sexuality as well, and to 'manage' my interactions with men more carefully. But I needed to learn that; perhaps it was like catch-up learning of what I should have learnt at university if I had been in a more normal environment. During this time I found I started to over-eat slightly. I wasn't bingeing, I was just using chocolate to soothe me or nurture me.

I remember needing to snap myself out of saying, 'I'm not going to let them destroy me or damage me!' I could see I was being self-destructive and expressing my lowered sense of self-worth through abusing my body. I went back to reminding myself: lists of good things done, three good meals, allow yourself a 'bad thing' each day, get in touch with yourself and your needs and your plans. I knew the culture or environment was affecting me again and had to keep telling myself not to be distracted by it.

As time went on I learned more to listen to my stomach and if I heard a voice saying, 'chocolate milk' I'd tend to indulge it. I became very satisfied at being 'in tune' with my body's needs, meeting them rather than denying them. I remember it actually took me several years to work out what food I liked; I was so out of tune with my body that I'd had years of never thinking about food in a normal manner. It took longer before I became equally good at listening to the 'I'm full' sign. It's funny, it was as if I had to re-earn the body's trust that I wasn't going to starve it or deny it again.

For me, bulimia was a result of my being too naïve and young and believing the irrational and harsh views of the culture I was in. My slight lack of self-esteem and dependence upon external success to be validated as a person made me more susceptible to believing the culture. Once I was emotionally and physiologically embroiled in the bulimia world it was very hard and a long process to break free. It was like breaking one tendril of a massive octopus at a time. Intellectual understanding was not enough to break the pattern; I needed to do activities that forced me to break instinctive and ingrained patterns of behaviour. I now see how important it is that young women have a robust sense of self-worth and a good understanding of 'who they are' before they encounter the world. Travelling the world after school or being given the freedom to try different courses or jobs to help 'find themselves' is worthwhile if self-knowledge is achieved.

In summary, I now do feel cured. I look back and shudder at the experience and am so glad I reached out for help and was lucky to be put on to a good counsellor. Throughout this the military was discreet and I visited Carole whenever we arranged to and the military just paid the bills without question. I have since found out that since I had what the military termed a mental disorder, going by the book they could have kicked me out. I was lucky this didn't happen. In discussions with other female graduates of that era, most commented that nearly every girl there had an eating disorder of some kind although none would ever admit to having one or to what extent they suffered. The military has changed a lot now and as a more senior member I am aware of such issues and am in a position to address cultural problems and 'look after' or keep an eye on the plight of the younger girls.

Introduction

...it's important that therapists know that anorexia and bulimia have to be dealt with on a number of different levels, that you can't just focus on the individual. What's happening for them or what's happening in the family or what's happening in the environment or society is all important together. You have to deal with it on all levels or else you are dealing with just part of what the problem is and I think it'll always come back if you don't (Letter from bulimic woman; Epston and Madigan 1995, p.8).

Introduction to the problem: Diagnostic criteria and definitions

The 'thin ideal' and weight dissatisfaction

In a society where food is abundant, it is not surprising that the average weight of women has increased. Yet the weight of the ideal body type, as portrayed in the media, has actually decreased (Logue 1991; Murphy 1997). While many women know that the 'thin ideal' is unrealistic, they remain unhappy with their body weight and shape (Stevens and Tiggemann 1998). This is because the 'thin ideal' has come to symbolise success, social status, wealth and self-discipline (Stice and Shaw 1994). Weight has become a quick and tangible measure of women's self-worth, desirability and ranking in relation to other women (Lacey and Birtchnell 1985).

Young women: a vulnerable group

Young women are more dissatisfied with their weight than women at any other stage of the female life span. Young women anxiously want to be socially accepted; they think they will be penalised socially if they are overweight (Tiggeman and Rothblum 1988) and rewarded, both personally and socially, if they achieve their 'thin ideal' weight (Klesges, Mizes and Klesges 1987). Therefore, they are more vulnerable to the enticing messages about the 'thin ideal' that the media conveys (Martin and Gentry 1997). Many young women get the message and resort to dieting in order to conform to current ideal weight standards. Dieting can quickly develop into an intense preoccupation with weight, that, in combination with other factors, turns into an eating disorder.

Thus, young women can change from having a normal relationship with food and eating to being obsessive about their weight and dieting. Some go on to develop an entrenched cycle of gorging and purging (bulimia nervosa). Others will literally starve themselves to death (anorexia nervosa). Some will swing between the two conditions, recovering from a bout of anorexia nervosa only to fall into the eating and vomiting pattern of bulimia nervosa before teetering back into anorexia nervosa. While both conditions are of concern to therapists, this book focuses primarily on the scope, significance and treatment of bulimia nervosa. It is an important problem not only for younger women; its themes resonate for all women. The following two sections define bulimia nervosa by giving the current diagnostic criteria and by distinguishing it from associated eating disorders. In the section following these, I introduce the reader to the systemic therapeutic approach used to treat the problem.

Diagnostic criteria for bulimia nervosa

The American Psychiatric Association's Diagnostic and Statistical Manual of Mental Disorders (DSM-IV; 1994) cites six definite criteria for diagnosing bulimia nervosa. The first criterion is recurrent episodes of binge-eating, that is, the rapid consumption of a large amount of food in a limited period of time, typically a two-hour time period. The quantity of food eaten is quite distinct from the common understanding of 'over-eating'. It is not unusual to hear that a woman with bulimia nervosa has consumed a bucket of ice cream, several chocolate bars, a packet of biscuits and the remnants of last night's meal including large scoops of left-over fat on top of a full meal. The second criterion given by DSM-IV is a feeling of lack of control over eating behaviour during eating binges. This is the feeling that one cannot stop eating or control what or how much one is eating. The third criterion is recurrent inappropriate compensatory behaviour in order to prevent weight gain. This may mean regular engagement in self-induced vomiting, misuse of laxatives, diuretics, enemas or other medications, strict dieting, fasting, or vigorous, excessive exercise. Women with bulimia are often categorised as those who purge (self-induced vomiting, laxatives and so on) and those who do not purge but rather, use inappropriate fasting or exercise. The fourth criterion specifies a minimum average of two binge-eating episodes a week for at least three months in order for the client to be diagnosed with the problem and the fifth criterion cites a persistent over-concern with body shape and weight. The bulimic client usually has a negative body image and a strong dissatisfaction with body size as well as a perceptual distortion of her body. The final criterion distin-guishes between bulimia nervosa and a variant of anorexia nervosa where there are bingeing and purging episodes. DSM-IV specifies that the bulimic behaviour does not occur exclusively during periods of anorexia nervosa.

Distinguishing between bulimia nervosa and associated eating disorders

It is only recently that bulimia nervosa has been clearly defined. While the Greek root of the word, *boulimos,* meaning 'ox hunger' is clearly traced, it is not as easy to track the condition through the maze of terms used in the psychological, medical and health-related literature. The condition is variously called the bulimic syndrome, compulsive eating, bulimarexia, the dietary chaos syndrome and the binge-purge syndrome. In addition, bulimia nervosa has often been confused with both anorexia nervosa and binge-eating disorder.

Anorexia nervosa, the self-starvation syndrome, has among its diagnostic criteria a lack of self-esteem; a paralysing sense of ineffectiveness; a distorted body image; an obsessive concern with food; and an extreme aversion to eating. However, in times of stress, those with bulimia nervosa turn *towards* food, not *away* from it. Unlike those with anorexia nervosa, in the later stages of their illness those with bulimia nervosa can still function in social and work contexts, albeit with difficulty.

Similarly, binge-eating disorder is characterised by recurrent episodes of binge-eating. However, unlike bulimia nervosa, extreme methods of weight control are absent (Wilson and Fairburn 1998).

Further, the DSM diagnostic criteria for scientific classification have changed over time, specifying more precisely the frequency and severity levels for classification. The way in which the frequency and severity levels have changed will be covered further in the epidemiological section in Chapter One. It is important to emphasise here, though, that such changes affect our interpretation of evidence from earlier epidemiological records, research reports and case histories.

If we take the existing evidence at face value, there are a number of effective treatments for bulimia nervosa, anorexia nervosa and binge-eating disorder. It is beyond the scope of this book to review the treatments for anorexia nervosa and binge-eating disorder (see Wilson and Fairburn 1998); it focuses exclusively on the use of systemic therapy for bulimia nervosa, because it incorporates the best of other evidence-based treatments and it addresses the needs of the client within the interconnecting systems within which she lives. In the following section, I introduce the systemic therapeutic approach to bulimia nervosa, describing the main ideas underpinning practice, and providing a rationale for its use.

Introduction to systemic therapy

A description of systemic therapy

In working with women of different ages and backgrounds, I have found systemic principles and practices to be effective in the treatment of bulimia nervosa. Many of these derive from systems theory and cybernetics, two theoretical frameworks that have been very influential in the practice of family therapy. According to the main principles of systemic therapy, individuals are viewed as nested within interconnected systems (individual, family or peer group, community and society). For those women who suffer from bulimia nervosa, these systems can cause and maintain the problem. For example, a young woman might diet and then binge in pursuit of the 'thin ideal'. Peer group pressure exacerbates these behaviours as does a tendency to rigidity in the way that a young woman thinks about herself. Her parents might unwittingly perpetuate the diet/binge cycle by also concentrating on her weight.

Each system can interact with other systems: for example, disgust with herself over the binge/purge behaviour can reduce her self-esteem and make her more susceptible to peer pressure. Because systemic therapy emphasises interaction and holism, it can address the major aspects of these systems as they pertain to bulimia nervosa – behavioural, interpersonal, developmental and sociocultural. It is important that it recognises and treats the central issue of control that has been found to connect all the aspects of the systems. Although various schools have developed within systemic therapy, there are common principles and practices that address these aspects and fit within an integrated framework. This book presents this framework and shows the way in which it can be used to guide the treatment of bulimia nervosa.

Rationale for systemic therapy

There are many therapeutic approaches to the treatment of bulimia nervosa, including cognitive-behavioural, psychodynamic, interpersonal and systemic (for a review of these approaches, see Wilson and Fairburn 1998). These different approaches define and treat different aspects of the problem. For example, cognitive-behavioural approaches view the problem as one of cognitive and behavioural maladjustment and therefore address the irrational self-talk and addictive behaviours of bulimia. Psychodynamic approaches emphasise the underlying and unresolved intrapsychic dynamics and work to explore these in analysis; and interpersonal therapy considers the problem to be one of interpersonal maladjustment and therefore uses problem-solving to work on the client's relationships.

Systemic therapy is my treatment of choice for bulimia nervosa for two sets of reasons. The first set concerns the 'good fit' between the multidimensional nature of bulimia nervosa and the multiple perspectives of systemic therapy. This therapy considers all the different aspects of bulimia nervosa, acknowledging the issue of control. The second set of reasons concerns systemic therapy's focus on individual needs. As a wide-ranging therapy, it has the potential to target treatment to the individual, rather than fit the individual to a model of treatment.

The first set: A good fit

First, systemic therapy, itself being multidimensional, can address the multidimensional nature of bulimia nervosa. Systemic therapies encourage alternative perspectives (an 'and-also' approach) to problems and are therefore inclusive of other treatments. They have the potential to incorporate the best evidence-based treatments, even those treatments that at first seem contradictory. For example, both cognitive-behavioural and interpersonal therapies are judged equally effective in treating bulimia nervosa; both achieve the same modest level of improvement at follow-up and have the same remission rate – approximately 40 per cent (for a review of these studies, see Wilson and Fairburn 1998). Yet, these therapies have very different aims and treatment plans. Systemic therapy, as an inclusive therapy, views both therapies as useful in addressing different aspects of bulimia nervosa. Preliminary findings from the use of systemic therapy with bulimia nervosa indicate a 60 per cent improvement with a corresponding remission rate (Kayrooz 1991).

Systemic therapy allows the clinician to explore multidimensional aspects of bulimia nervosa in treating the problem, including interpersonal and sociocultural aspects as well as the customary behavioural and cognitive aspects. In comprehensively addressing all aspects of the problem, systemic therapies acknowledge that treating any one aspect to the exclusion of others may inadvertently entrench the problem. If only one aspect of the problem is addressed, then the other aspects may undo the benefits that result.

For example, consider a young woman who undergoes cognitive-behavioural treatment in an eating disorder clinic. When she leaves the safety of the context of the clinic, she may become exposed to the family and peer pressures and tensions and relapse once again. Her relapse may further diminish her sense of self-worth, making it even more difficult for her to break free from the problem. While the use of cognitive-behavioural therapy will address her self-talk and addictive behaviours, it may not address the family and peer pressures on the outside, nor the tensions arising from important life decisions.

Treating all aspects of bulimia nervosa is also important because it avoids wasting effort in castigating others for causing or maintaining the problem. If bulimia nervosa is multiply determined, then it is not caused by any single person or event such as the actions of family members or personality factors. Without a focus on any particular cause of the problem, there is no one person or event to blame for the problem. The perception that an individual can control any system is an illusion that can lead to wasted effort in surmounting the problem. Awareness of all aspects will allow both therapist and client to find points within the overall system that have the potential to leverage maximal change. Resultant changes should ripple out to all other parts of the overall system.

Systemic therapy also allows therapists to emphasise important sociocultural aspects that develop and maintain the bulimia nervosa. There are many reasons for highlighting sociocultural aspects: eating disorders are more frequent in groups which stress the importance of thinness; the problem is less common among white non-Caucasians although it increases dramatically for those who are acculturating to white Caucasian society (Bhadrinath 1990; Nasser 1988; Nevo 1985); the 'thin ideal' typically applies only to women; women account for approximately 95 per cent of eating disorders; and over the past 20 years, there has been a greater discrepancy between women's actual and ideal weights corresponding to concomitant increases in women's body dissatisfaction, eating disorders and depression (Kenny and Adams 1994).

The sociocultural causal chain is straightforward and strong for bulimia nervosa. The portrayal of the 'thin ideal' in the media encourages weight dissatisfaction in women (Stevens and Tiggemann 1998). Weight dissatisfaction is a powerful precursor to dieting, which, in turn, can lead to bulimic episodes (Monteath and McCabe 1997; Murphy 1997). Given the clear linkages between weight dissatisfaction, dieting and the development of bulimia nervosa, it is surprising to find that not all therapeutic approaches give due emphasis to sociocultural aspects. Two common evidence-based treatments, cognitive-behavioural and interpersonal therapy, emphasise very different aspects. Cognitive-behavioural therapy focuses on the role of both cognitive and behavioural factors in the maintenance of bulimia nervosa and therefore the treatment aims to address dysfunctional thoughts and attitudes about body shape and weight and to replace dietary restraint with more normal eating patterns. In contrast, interpersonal therapy does not specifically address weight-related behaviours, rather it focuses on the skills needed to change problems that the client is having currently with friends, peers and others (Arnow 1999).

Contrary to the current view that women with bulimia are maladjusted to society, the systemic view is that the society is as much a 'poor fit' for the individual. If we only treat personality and behavioural aspects that predispose individuals to bulimia nervosa, we may de-emphasise the serious harm that is done to young women by continual exposure to media images of an impossibly 'thin ideal'. By acknowledging the sociocultural aspects, systemic therapy can call for cultural accountability for bulimia nervosa and endorse social action and preventive interventions, such as educational programmes and governmental regulations. These ultimately attempt to redress the destructive aspects of the culture for women.

In summary, systemic therapy matches the multidimensional nature of bulimia nervosa, appropriately highlighting the sociocultural aspects. Because it is itself multidimensional, systemic therapy has the potential to incorporate the best of other treatment approaches. Because bulimia nervosa is multiply determined, blame is not a useful concept for either the therapist or the client; nor is a sense of unilateral and rigid control useful over any aspect of the systems within which the individual is embedded. The following set of reasons shows how systemic therapy assists the therapist to select relevant aspects and to integrate these into a workable treatment plan targeted to the specific needs of the individual (Haynes, Huland-Spain and Oliviera 1993). As such, systemic therapies reduce the rigidity dictated by the use of model treatments, allowing a more accurate fit between the treatment plan and the individual's needs.

The second set: individual needs

The second set of reasons draws our attention to this potential to tailor a treatment plan to the needs of the individual. There is evidence to suggest that therapists can seek information that confirms their preconceptions about the client, selectively process client information and distort information that arises from the client's presentation and the context of that information (for example, see Arkes 1991; Evans 1989). Comprehensive differentiation of the various aspects and themes of the problem avoids therapeutic bias and allows a focus on the individual, by making maximum use of all available and relevant information (Arkes 1991; Green 1990; Hirt and Markman 1995; Keren 1990; Nezu and Nezu 1993).

Related to the ability to be comprehensive, systemic therapy has the potential to increase therapist empathy, one of the most important variables for effective treatment; if the therapist uses a comprehensive approach, he or she will come to understand the client's experience in its complexity and uniqueness (McLennan, Twigg and Bezant 1993). Unidimensional judgements of the client (for example, functional/ dysfunctional, rigid/flexible) will be suspended so that the myriad views of the client and the people and events in her life allow spontaneous unguarded exploration. Thus a comprehensive understanding of the problem will assist the therapist to increase the rapport with the client and to strengthen the client's often impoverished perspectives. In two often-cited meta-analytic studies that examined therapeutic effectiveness (Shapero and Shapero 1982; Smith and Glass 1977), therapy outcome was predicted by the quality of the therapeutic relationship as determined by the therapist's personal characteristics (Herman 1993). My argument here is that the comprehensiveness of systemic therapy allows a greater appreciation of the complexity of both the individual and the problem, leading to greater empathy.

In recognising the unique nature of the individual, systemic therapy can access her strengths. Many women with the problem have commented on the 'totalising' effect of the label of 'bulimic', as though this label represents the sum total of their being. They have felt the label to be disempowering, lessening other qualities that they felt they possessed. One of the main interventions of systemic therapy is the use of forgotten but cherished qualities to highlight possible solutions to the problem. Systemic therapy acknowledges the individuality of the client, accentuating the positive qualities and aspects of her personality and life. As one client noted,

> When they (therapists) look at you as a bulimic person, you begin to look at yourself that way to [sic]. You begin to identify purely with your anorexia and your bulimia and you lose your self... every-time people and professionals (focus just on the bulimia) you become smaller and smaller. (I began to get better when I) separated bulimia from myself... (and saw it as) one aspect of myself and just that (Epston and Madigan 1995, p.8).

In summary, the second set of reasons shows that systemic therapy has the potential to counteract therapeutic bias about the nature of the problem and can increase empathy because it allows a more comprehensive view of the problem, the client and the impact of the problem in the client's life. In paying close attention to the individual, the therapist can note the client's strengths and then use these to find possible solutions to the problem.

The book and its structure

This book is intended as both a resource and a thematic and pragmatic guide to working with women with bulimia nervosa. It will be useful for those with an interest in systemic therapy and those interested in bulimia nervosa. The research on bulimia nervosa is given and the main themes that emerge during therapy are defined and illustrated in case studies. The stages of treatment, therapeutic practices and general session guidelines (shown to be effective, and which address the research and the clinical themes) are proposed. I hope this book helps the psychologist, counsellor and social worker practising in the field to understand, and aid, the predominantly female population suffering from bulimia nervosa.

In Chapter One, I introduce the reader to the scope and significance of bulimia nervosa, thereby providing a background to the problem. This chapter covers the history and ethnography of bulimia nervosa, and its prevalence, pharmacology and probable aetiology. It also shows the therapist the likely general trends in clients who come to therapy, taking care to acknowledge the unique aspects of each individual. Chapter Two shows the themes that emerge in the analysis of processes during therapy. These themes are behavioural, interpersonal, developmental and sociocultural aspects. The issue of control runs, like a connecting band, through them. This issue will be revisited at several points during the book to underscore its centrality. The content of Chapter Two is based on experience with the difficulties young women face as they try to surmount the problem. I propose that the successful treatment of bulimia nervosa requires careful path-finding through the therapeutic terrain formed by the themes and the central issue of control that emerges from them. Systemic therapy addresses each of the themes and the central issue, guiding the therapist and client through this complex terrain.

Chapter Three describes the overall stages of treatment for bulimia nervosa using systemic therapy. The therapeutic themes are sequenced to structure the flow of sessions across the course of therapy. In Chapter Four, specific tasks and interventions are given that are used to address the themes. Care has been taken to balance the type of tasks and interventions with the four main thematic aspects of the problem – behavioural, interpersonal, developmental and sociocultural. In Chapter Five, general procedures provide a guide for the therapist within each session. Chapters Six, Seven and Eight illustrate the themes in the context of specific cases. An analysis of these processes in therapy as presented in the case studies reveals the themes explored in Chapter Two as well as the generalised and specific practices that enable recovery in Chapters Three and Four. Chapter Nine analyses these practices and proposes possible reasons, from a systems-based perspective, for their effectiveness. This final chapter summarises the main themes and the central issue in therapy, that of power and control, and gathers together the therapeutic practices that enable the therapist to address this issue in therapy.

In order to assist women with bulimia nervosa, it is necessary to understand the scope and significance of the problem. Besides showing the history and ethnography of the problem, the next chapter reviews the prevalence, probable causes and medical effects of bulimia nervosa.

CHAPTER ONE

Scope and Significance of Bulimia Nervosa

There is a wealth of evidence on the scope, causes and consequences of bulimia nervosa. The therapist needs to be intelligently informed (and critical) about general patterns of occurrence of the problem, and the personal, familial and medical profiles of clients who present for therapy. Such information will assist the therapist to prepare for both common client responses and any contingencies. In this chapter, I review and critically examine the scope and significance of bulimia nervosa. The evidence on its prevalence, aetiology, and pharmacology is presented and the typical course of the problem is illustrated with a model. The common risk factors for developing the problem are identified throughout. By way of an introduction to the scope and significance of bulimia nervosa, I begin by briefly outlining the problem's history and ethnography.

The history and ethnography of bulimia nervosa

Bulimia nervosa through the ages

According to some historians (and contrary to current thinking in the eating disorder literature), eating disorder symptoms have existed for some time. There have been accounts of problems resembling bulimia recorded during ancient and medieval times (Crowther, Wolf and Sherwood 1992). The ancient Egyptians thought that food could cause disease and they purged on a monthly basis. The Romans used vomitoriums to eliminate their excesses. During the Middle Ages, religious people engaged in severe purification fasts sometimes of long duration, eating only enough to sustain life.

While the behaviour was considered normal in these accounts, other accounts from physicians during ancient times show that 'boulimos' or 'ox hunger' was certainly problematic (Ziolko 1996). There are accounts from Asclepiades, a Greek physician practising in Rome in the first century BC, of patients who took nourishment day and night. Boulimos was also documented by the lexicographers of the first century AD. Other accounts come from Roman physicians of the fourth century in North Africa, writing about an 'extraordinary desire to eat'. By 1000AD, boulimos came to mean a constant, insatiable, inordinately great hunger. Greek physicians in the seventh century noted patients' typical oscillation from boulimos to self-starvation. Other accounts, from case notes and studies, anecdotes and clinical files, exist throughout the centuries bringing us up to the present time.

The first modern scientific description of anorexia nervosa occurred in 1887 when Gull documented cases of 'nervous loss of appetite'. It took approximately another century for Stunkard, in 1959, to describe binge-eating, by documenting cases of uncontrolled eating. Twenty years later, in 1979, Russell gave the first scientific descriptions of bulimia nervosa in his article 'Bulimia nervosa: an ominous variant of anorexia nervosa'. Thus, while the problem has only recently been identified scientifically in the literature, it is possible that bulimia nervosa has existed for some time. However, it is also possible that the frequency and severity of the problem has increased in modern times.

An increase in the problem: the advent of industrialisation
Some theorists have suggested that the number of eating disorder cases increased during the advent of industrialisation (Littlewood 1995). They have linked women's fear of fatness with extreme economic and public health changes. With industrialisation, there was a radical departure from foraging and farming as major activities.

Accordingly, eating became divorced from survival for many people. Food access became more secure at the same time as people became separated from the means of production. Eating began to develop as a leisure activity and food preparation and consumption signified, even more strongly, one's class and status in the society. Some researchers (for example, Littlewood 1995) have speculated that women needed to distance themselves from food preparation in order to be perceived as having the ability to occupy different roles. Some have noted that women were increasingly required to diet to gain access to employment and to educational and economic resources.

Cross-cultural comparisons

In contrast, in non-industrialised societies where access to food was not reliable, women's relative plumpness signified health, prosperity and fertility (Littlewood 1995). There are many documented cases showing that eating disorders are much less common among non-white Caucasians and less industrialised peoples (for example, Bhadrinath 1990; Nasser 1988; Nevo 1985). In less industrialised societies, eating disorders generally tend to occur among the daughters of urban entrepreneurs and the professional elite who have been exposed to western mores (Littlewood 1995). Among non-European minorities newly arrived in the West, there are generally fewer negative connotations of female obesity, less preoccupation with personal weight loss and a lower prevalence of bulimia nervosa (Davis and Yager 1992). There is growing evidence, however, that these differences disappear as the minority group adjusts to the culture of the host country (Davis and Katzman 1999). In some instances (for example, Egyptian and Asian women in England), where this acculturation process causes extreme dissonance for young women, there are even higher rates of eating disorder symptoms than for the local population (Littlewood 1995).

Cultural role conflict: a theory of eating disorders

Cultural role conflict is thought to lead to the high level of eating disorders among those who need to adjust to the dominant western culture (Littlewood 1995; Nasser 1997). According to this theory, the immigrant woman, by means of the eating disorder, can express distress about the conflict between the greater personal freedoms offered by the host culture and the restrictions of her culture of origin, without overtly challenging her culture of origin's norms. In this sense, the disorder comes to represent role confusion and social dislocation. Littlewood (1995) suggests that the eating disorder can function in a similar manner to culturally-accepted dissociative states, such as spirit possession, that occurred in non-industrialised societies for centuries. According to this view, the eating disorder gives the woman permission to express the previously taboo sense of personal agency or freedom; others can then attribute her demands safely to some external force. These kinds of sociocultural explanations for the occurrence of the problem will be explored further in this chapter and the next.

Developmental crises and other societies

It is interesting to compare women's developmental crises to developmental crises in other societies, both cross-culturally and longitudinally. The formality of rites of passage in non-industrial societies may provide better definition of people's place in that society and the demands of their new roles. It is not unusual for adolescents in non-industrial societies to move through periods of disordered relationships with food. Certain foods will be taboo or prepared in a special way and the teenager excluded from everyday society and guided through initiation by designated elders. Perhaps a fanciful explanation of bulimic behaviour is associated with the unguided restrictions and excesses typical of these passages that are still being played out unsuccessfully in our society. Certainly, studies on adolescents and young women in industrialised societies (for example, Abraham et al. 1983) show that disordered eating patterns are characteristic of a sizeable proportion of late adolescents

Continual disintegration of societal roles may lead to a situation where excess and restriction become permanent features of that society. An even more fanciful explanation of bulimia nervosa is suggested by the work of Arnold Toynbee (1972). His depiction of the disintegration of civilisations – Hellenic, Egyptian, Syriac and Roman – includes a description of the psychological schisms which individuals unfortunate enough to be born into such eras undergo. Two types of personal behaviour mark these historical epochs and both are substitutes for creative expression: an abandon 'in which the soul lets itself go utterly, believing that creativeness comes as the reward of a natural and wholly undisciplined spontaneity' (p.211) and a rigorous restraint of the natural passions through an ascetic life of self-denial.

As a metaphor of society's disintegration, bulimia nervosa embodies the utter abandon and stoic self-denial that is reminiscent of social collapse. However, while Toynbee (1972) argues for a dialectic of disintegration, the maelstrom created by the disintegration being the font of new life, no such analysis befits the metaphor of bulimia nervosa. Many clients, no doubt, would wonder what new life could possibly be gained from the very private maelstrom that often engulfs them.

In summary, eating disorder symptoms have existed for some time, although they probably increased in frequency and severity after industrialisation. The evidence for this is that there are fewer documented cases in less industrialised societies today, except in those sections of the society that are exposed to western mores. The general explanation for the higher occurrence is that individuals exposed to western values experience fewer guidelines for role transitions, and greater role conflict, some expressing this inner conflict in a disordered relationship with food and inflexible response to transitionary periods. The following section provides further background to the occurrence of bulimia nervosa in our society by outlining the evidence on its prevalence and incidence.

Epidemiology

A preliminary caution

There have been few studies of the prevalence and incidence of bulimia nervosa (Hamilton 1999). Of those that exist, there are four reasons to be cautious in interpreting their results. First, bulimia nervosa is hard to estimate because the standard diagnostic criteria have varied since it was first scientifically described (Hoek 1993). Surveys of the incidence and prevalence of bulimia nervosa have used three different criteria for classifications DSM-III, DSM-IIIR, and DSM-IV, leading to evidence in research reports that is based on different diagnoses (Allen, Scannel and Turner 1998; Levey, McDermott and Lee 1989). For example, the recent restrictive criteria of DSM-IV for classification (for example, two or more weekly binges for a three month period) has reduced prevalence rates in some studies by over 50 per cent (Hamilton 1999). Second, surveys often cover a number of other eating disorders such as 'bulimia' or binge-eating (Hamilton 1999), not sufficiently distinguishing them from bulimia nervosa. This lack of clarity of definition coupled to loose terminology in the health literature further confounds the evidence on the prevalence and incidence of the problem. Third, the prevalence of bulimia nervosa is difficult to determine because many, if not most, individuals suffering from this condition are extremely secretive about their behaviour and are unlikely to divulge information during an interview or even an anonymous survey (Blinder and Chao 1994; Touyz and Beumont 1985). Finally, the course of bulimia nervosa is quite different from anorexia nervosa. With anorexia nervosa, the condition becomes apparent over time, whereas with bulimia nervosa, women can often look and function normally at work and play for quite some time, making detection difficult.

The problem predominantly affects women

Despite these cautions, it is accepted that bulimia nervosa mostly affects white middle- and upper-class women (Fairburn and Beglin 1990). Within Caucasian societies, only approximately 5 to 10 per cent of all people with the problem are males (Striegal-Moore 1992).

There are reports, however, that some males seem to mask the problem under fitness regimes (Carlat and Camargo 1991). There is also some evidence that males, in response to increasing cultural pressures for attractiveness, may be catching up with women in terms of dissatisfaction with their bodies (Braun, Sunday, Huang and Halmi 1999; Mislkind *et al.* 1986). As weight dissatisfaction is seen to be a trigger for bulimic behaviour, this may, in turn, increase the likelihood that men will develop eating disorders in greater numbers. While treatment for male bulimia is important for practitioners, most identified patients are female. The focus of this book, then, is on treatment of females with bulimia nervosa, particularly young women. The research shows that adolescent and young adult females are more dissatisfied with their bodies and have higher drives for thinness than older females and nearly all males. It is important to note that even the most overweight males are more satisfied with their bodies than the most underweight females (Kenny and Adams 1994).

Bulimia nervosa: a substantial problem

Despite my cautions about interpreting the evidence that were expressed above, bulimia nervosa seems to be a substantial problem in our society and one that may be increasing. While reviews of the prevalence of bulimia nervosa in various western countries can range from 1 per cent to 19 per cent, reliable estimates of the incidence are typically two per cent or below (Fairburn and Beglin 1990; Stein 1991). It is worth noting that these figures approximate the incidence of both anorexia nervosa and clinical depression (Hamilton 1999). Four large-scale surveys from the UK (King 1989), the US (Whitaker *et al.* 1989), New Zealand (Hall and Hay 1991) and Australia (Kenny and Adams 1994) have all obtained similar prevalence rates for both bulimia nervosa and anorexia. Further, while little work has been done to estimate death from bulimia nervosa, there is preliminary evidence that the problem has a crude mortality rate of about 0.3 per cent (Keel and Mitchell 1997, 1999).

While there has been some contention in the literature as to whether the problem is increasing (see Heatherton *et al.* 1995;

Kendler *et al.* 1991), there are other studies to suggest that this is the case (Furnham and Patel 1994). A 20-year Swiss study showed the incidence of anorexia nervosa for females between 12 and 25 years had increased four-fold for that age range (Touyz and Beumont 1985). Another more recent Australian study showed prevalence rates of bulimia nervosa in a sample of 13- to 30-year-old women to be between 5 and 8 per cent (Hamilton 1999) – that is, over twice the general prevalence rate.

Sub-clinical aspects

The general prevalence rate is certainly higher in studies that include sub-clinical aspects of the disorder, such as over-concern with weight (King 1989). When sub-clinical aspects of the disorder were included in large-scale surveys, female prevalence rates in a general population rose to 4 per cent (King 1989). Similar rates for the prevalence of sub-clinical aspects of between 3 and 5 per cent have been reported for British female college and university students (Button and Whitehouse 1981; Clarke and Palmer 1983) and for British school girls (Szmukler 1983). The most common aspect is over-concern with weight, the extent of which is staggering, particularly among the young. When concerns about weight and other individual symptoms were included in surveys of 13- to 30-year-olds, the results showed widespread dissatisfaction with weight (Hamilton 1999); 70–80 per cent wished to lose weight (Dwyer *et al.* 1969; Ryan and Roughan 1984); and 60–73 per cent reported that they had at some stage felt fat and consciously tried to limit their food intake (Abraham *et al.* 1983). In a study of a high school population, 63 per cent of 1373 high school girls were dieting on the day of the study despite the fact that most of these adolescents were already at a normal weight level. Even 18 per cent of the underweight girls in this survey were trying to lose weight (Rosen and Gross 1989)! In a study of young children, 50 per cent of third to sixth grade (eight to twelve years) boys and girls wanted to weigh less and 16 per cent reported attempting weight loss (Schur, Sanders and Steiner 2000).

There is evidence that many young women pass through a stage of disordered eating which some suggest may be considered part of 'normal' western development. An early Australian study (Abraham *et al.* 1983) examined the eating and weight control behaviours of four groups of young women between 15 and 27 years of age (106 school and university students, 50 ballet dancers, 22 patients suffering from anorexia nervosa and 44 patients with bulimia). The results suggested that most young women dieted at some time; they may go through episodes of binge-eating and 'picking' behaviour and they generally wished to be thinner irrespective of their body weight. The Abraham *et al.* (1983) study suggests that 20 per cent of young women may fulfil the criteria (except those of duration) for an eating disorder – bulimia nervosa or anorexia nervosa – at some stage, however briefly, and about 7 per cent abuse laxatives or diuretics in order to achieve a fashionably slim figure. Studies with high school, college and university populations generally suggest much higher estimates of the incidence of bulimia nervosa with this population. In the Australian context, Touyz (1984) has estimated the prevalence of bulimia nervosa in the university student population as being somewhere between 6.9 per cent and 18 per cent. Hamilton, Meade and Gelwick (1980) cite an approximate figure of eight per cent of the total female undergraduate population. Generally, the estimates of these populations vary in the literature between 5 and 23 per cent (Levey, McDermott and Lee 1989). These high percentages are sobering when one considers the possibility of many being caught in the vortex of bulimia nervosa.

While the above figures once again highlight the importance of sociocultural factors such as weight dissatisfaction and dieting, these alone are not sufficient to account for the development of an eating disorder. A wide range of personality, developmental and familial variables are also documented and possibly play a role in predisposing people to the problem. For example, Patton *et al.* (1990) found that the risk of developing an eating disorder in dieting adolescents increased eight-fold when other psychiatric symptoms were present.

In the following sections, I will examine the typical personality and familial profiles for women with bulimia nervosa. Knowledge of these kinds of characteristic patterns should alert therapists to their clients' typical worries and concerns, thereby increasing therapists' empathy. Such information is not intended to reduce the client to a set of symptoms or a typical profile, but rather to provide more information about probable patterns in the client's life so that a treatment plan can be targeted to her specific needs.

Aetiology

A model of the development of bulimia nervosa

Bulimia nervosa has a gradual creeping history very much like that of substance abuse. Bulimia nervosa rarely begins with the full-blown binge and purge cycle. Often, women begin to diet after noticing that they have gained weight or after experiencing some dissatisfaction with body shape (Brouwers 1990). The adolescent or young woman who has gained weight often feels the pressure to be thin from family, friends and media. This pressure then leads her to further internalise the thin ideal, to feel dissatisfied with her own body, and to diet. This weight dissatisfaction and subsequent dieting seems to be a precondition for bingeing then purging which leads, for some, to the development of bulimia nervosa (Hart and Chiovari 1998; Huon 1994; Polivy and Herman 1985).

Perhaps she hears from print or word of mouth about purging or perhaps it is something she thinks of doing quite spontaneously. At first, only occasionally does she try to counteract the negative effects of a binge by purging. At these early stages, the binge-purge episodes represent interruptions in an otherwise normal life, but failure to lose weight can lead to a worsened sense of self-esteem.

Over time, the attacks on her self-esteem caused by the failure to stop bingeing and purging are likely to generalise to chronic depression or anxiety. With repeated bingeing and purging, the individual gradually grows insensitive to internal sensations of hunger; cognitive cues to control food intake take on more significance than both internal and external cues. Chronic restraint then leads to further binges. Purging is an attempt to regain self-control but instead it gradually leads to a sense of dissociation. Many describe the sense of release and of 'new beginnings' immediately following a purge and the accompanying rise in self-esteem. This is usually followed by a resolution to stop bingeing forever. Many think that total abstinence from forbidden or taboo foods is the only acceptable way of gaining control, dooming the bulimic to swing between rigid control and complete chaos.

She often finds that life difficulties result in yet more purging. Continued exposure to media images of the 'thin ideal' might then maintain the problem because she typically overestimates her size and diets further (Stice 1999). She begins to crave, then loses control and binges. She feels guilty, ashamed and disgusted with herself. However, fear of being fat means that she will purge again. Purging gives a semblance of control, but ultimately leads to tension (Weiss, Katzman and Wolchik 1994) and the cycle repeats again and again. Unfortunately, this stage of the development of the problem is often short-lived as the behaviour can increase in frequency and severity in a remarkably short time. Her life then becomes a perpetual diet accompanied by insatiable binges and purifying purges.

In the following sections, I explore some of the suggested causes for the development of the problem, beginning with the most important cause, our culture's espousal of the 'thin ideal' and women's common response, weight dissatisfaction and dieting. The evidence on personality and familial factors is outlined, together with some of the developmental challenges that seem to provoke the problem.

Society and the 'thin ideal'

Objectification theory is the main feminist theory explaining the mechanism whereby women develop bulimia nervosa (Fredrickson and Roberts 1997). Its main premise is that western culture encourages a sexualised gazing or visual inspection of women's bodies. This is principally promoted through the media, that is, television, billboards, posters and magazines. According to the theory, women's body parts or sexual functions are separated out from their identity and reduced to instruments for the use and pleasure of others. (Theorists acknowledge that men's bodies are also increasingly subjected to this gaze but disproportionately so, compared to women's.) This kind of inspection occurs both in actual interpersonal encounters and in the visual mass media. The cultural milieu of sexual objectification functions to encourage girls and women to treat themselves as objects and to be evaluated on the basis of appearance. Because others' evaluations of their looks can ultimately shape their social and economic life outcomes, women respond by attending to their physical appearance. They are well aware of the social repercussions of their appearance. Self-objectification leads to a form of vigilant self-consciousness that continuously monitors the body's outward appearance (Fredrickson et al. 1998). This, in turn, creates other consequences including shame at not measuring up to the culture's 'thin ideal', anxiety, a diminished awareness of one's internal body states, weight dissatisfaction and dieting. For some, eating disorders will result.

Objectification theory cogently explains how dissatisfaction is promoted to young women through sexualised gazing and how they come to feel devalued as a person. However, it does address the fact that the gazing involved in the 'thin ideal' is not primarily sexual but rather it is oriented towards fashion and status. If one views the sexual literature or sexualised advertisements, women's bodies are sexualised but they do not ascribe to the 'thin ideal'. In the research literature, men have been found consistently to prefer larger females. In contrast, if one views women's magazines, one is overwhelmed by emaciated young girls and women. In a recent documentary depicting the use of models in the major fashion houses in Milan, the fashion designers and their entourage appeared to be encouraging the svelte androgynous form for their misogynist ends. The strong implication was that many of the power brokers within the fashion industry were predominantly wanting sexual favours from under-age girls who looked like boys. These people did not like women nor the female form. Thus it may not be a sexual gazing that contributes to the development of bulimia nervosa but rather the impact of a misogynistic fashion world.

Personality factors

Women tend to develop extrinsic personality characteristics as a direct result of their desire to conform to the 'thin ideal'. Because the 'thin ideal' is an impossible goal for many women, those who ascribe to it tend to have low self-esteem, depression and anxiety and a high need for approval (McCarthy 1990). They also tend to feel socially undesirable. Some authors have suggested that continued failure at dieting results in shame and a diminished self-esteem, although an interesting survey of elementary and middle-school girls revealed other cultural causes of shame. According to this study, shame is brought about by several specific factors (Barr-Taylor *et al.* 1998).

For elementary school girls, shame arises from trying to look like girls and women on TV and in magazines. For middle-school girls (aged about 12 years), it arises in order of importance from the emphasis that peers place on weight and eating; their level of confidence; trying to look like girls and women on TV and in the magazines; and being teased about weight. It is interesting that the type of TV programme is a factor in producing shame. Soaps, movies, music and video segments positively have a drive for thinness in young women whereas sporting programmes negatively have this drive (Tiggeman and Pickering 1996).

There are other intrinsic personality characteristics that predispose women to bulimia nervosa. Women with this problem often have distinctive personality traits that can act as filters influencing their perception of their environment and their personal health. They can be predisposed to rigid patterns of thinking and behaviour, involving a preoccupation with weight, poor body image and an over-emphasis on physical appearance (Weiss *et al.* 1994). Rigid and dichotomised thinking is the most difficult pattern to break; women with the problem often have an 'either-or' approach to life which impoverishes its complexity, leaving them feeling helpless in situations demanding creative action.

There are a number of rigid patterns of thinking (see Root, Fallon and Friedrich 1986). They often feel that they must be approved of by everyone for everything they do, and that they should be in control and competent at all times. They feel responsible for everyone's feelings and that they should be considerate at all times. If anything goes wrong, they often believe it is their fault. Events need to go exactly as planned otherwise they think they are out of control. To some extent, these thinking patterns belong to most women with a sense of responsibility and compassion but in women with bulimia nervosa, they tend to be extreme. This is because women with this problem tend to be perfectionists (Woodman and Dickson 1996) and then guilty because they have not reached their own high goals (Allen, Scannel and Turner 1998).

They also tend to have more expressive traits. Expressive traits are stereotypically feminine and include being emotional, dependent, concerned for others, nurturing and communal. In contrast, instrumental traits are more stereotypically masculine and include being assertive, independent and self-expansionist – highly valued characteristics in western society. One international study showed that women with bulimia nervosa score higher on more expressive rather than instrumental traits (Shifren, Furnham and Bauserman 1998). Although these characteristics are typically considered to be fixed traits, the authors acknowledge that these traits do not exist in a vacuum; they develop within a family or cultural environment that reinforces the display of certain characteristics over others, ultimately shaping the development of those traits within males and females.

Expressive types tend to be quite passive in their orientation to the world. Women with bulimia similarly present as passive, with a strong desire to please and yet often distrustful and suspicious of others. Not expressing their needs may lead to covert hostility as they try to deal with conflicting emotions (Allen, Scannel and Turner 1998). As a result, bulimic women often have difficulties with interpersonal relationships. In conflict, they tend to use avoidance or attack strategies rather than assertively addressing problems.

Depression is also commonly linked with bulimia nervosa (Lenoux, Steiger and Jabalpurlawa 2000) although it is not known whether bulimia nervosa leads to endogenous depression (that is, depression caused by internal factors) or whether they have a common cause. Depression can become very severe, leading to suicidal thoughts and even attempts at suicide. Certainly, the more severe the bulimia in terms of length of time with the problem and frequency of binge-purge episodes the more severe the depression and the lack of self-esteem. There are similarities between women who are endogenously depressed and those who have bulimia nervosa. Bulimics have been shown to have abnormal results on the dexamethosone depression test, a test assessing unregulated cortico-steroid production. Approximately 20 to 60 per cent show abnormal results on it. The results suggest similarities in metabolic pathways between people with endogenous depression and women with bulimia (Kaplan, Garfinkel and Brown 1989). Accordingly, many bulimic symptoms have been shown to improve with the use of anti-depressants such as imipramine and Prozac (Pope *et al.* 1983) although the long-term effects of this sort of medication remain largely untested (Wilson and Fairburn 1998).

Besides the apparent similarity between bulimic and addictive patterns, there is evidence actually linking bulimia nervosa and alcoholism. Watts and Ellis (1992) found that 27 per cent of girls between the ages of 12 and 17 reported eating disorder symptoms and this was associated with greater frequency of alcohol consumption and greater volume consumed on each occasion. Although I have not experienced this association with my bulimic clients, this may be a pattern for which the therapist will need to be alert.

Familial characteristics

Many bulimics come from families with interpersonal difficulties. In one study, women diagnosed with bulimia nervosa were followed up over a ten-year period after diagnosis to determine the problem's long-term effect (Keel *et al.* 2000). While the bulimic symptoms decreased for these women, many showed continuing impairment in interpersonal relationships. There is also evidence that rates of affective disorders among close relatives are high as compared with close relatives of controls (people who do not have bulimic symptoms), approximately 30 per cent compared with 8 per cent in controls (Hatsukami *et al.* 1986).

Despite these high rates, it still remains unclear whether specific family interaction patterns partly contribute to the problem. Certainly, family relationships have received a lot of attention as risk factors for the onset and maintenance of anorexia nervosa (Minuchin, Rosman and Baker 1978; Selvini-Palazzoli *et al.* 1974; Selvini-Palazzoli *et al.* 1978). Using their clinical experience and early family therapy theory and research, Root, Fallon and Friedrich (1986) categorised three distinct types of families with symptomatic members – perfect, over-protective and chaotic. These three types were thought to characterise 'bulimic families', just as Minuchin (Munichin, Rosman and Baken 1978) had identified families with an anorectic member as 'anorectic families'. According to this view, bulimic families are dysfunctional and one member in them enacts the family's distress by manifesting symptoms.

The 'perfect' family has an emphasis on appearance, family reputation, family identity and achievement. There is an intense and enmeshed family loyalty, with members being faithful to family secrets and keeping family pain hidden. 'United we stand, divided we fall' is an epithet encapsulating this type of family. The 'over-protective' family is characterised by marital conflict and, generally, poor conflict resolution skills. There is a lack of recognition of the child's competence and her needs for independence. The feeling in the family is captured by the phrase 'no-one is really good enough for my daughter'. The 'chaotic' family has inconsistent rules, frequent expression of anger and even substance abuse. One or both parents are often physically and/or emotionally unavailable. 'The only one you can really count on is yourself' is an often-heard or understood feeling in this family. According to Root, Fallon and Friedrich (1986), the symptoms of bulimia nervosa provide a vehicle for the presenting client to be viewed separately and to express anger. They also enable the family to express distress.

The majority of these clinical impressions (for example, see Minuchin, Rosman and Baker 1978; Root, Fallon and Friedrich 1986; Selvini-Palazzoli *et al.* 1978) are often based on theory-driven considerations and clinical observation, not direct evidence. The results from several self-report family assessment instruments, however, suggest that bulimics, and to a lesser extent their parents, perceive their families to be less expressive, involved and cohesive, more conflicted, disorganised and achievement-oriented than do controls. Bulimic women see their families as more blaming, rejecting and neglectful and less nurturing and comforting than controls. Similarly, observational studies of families where a member is bulimic show the parents to be hostile and neglectful and the daughter to be 'angrily submissive' (for a review of these self-report and observational studies, see Wonderlich 1992).

Generally, studies on family functioning must be considered with some caution because of methodological weaknesses in the subjective collecting and recording of data and the wide variability of family functioning where a member has bulimia nervosa (Grigg, Friesen and Sheppy 1989). A perception of dysfunctional family tendencies could also be due to the distressed reaction of the family after finding out about the bulimic member. Valid studies of tendencies in family functioning should include predictive longitudinal data from a wide range of families of young women. To my knowledge, this research has not been undertaken.

Differences in family functioning where a member is bulimic may be due to any number of factors. For example, there may be differences in children's personalities leading to family discord or there may be a match or mismatch between parental and child characteristics. The consequences of family life transitions or indeed other peer-related or life experiences will also have an effect, so that ascribing cause to the family is unfair and, worse still, damaging. As Wonderlich (1992) noted in his review of the research on families of bulimics, future family studies of bulimia should also consider the unique environments that bulimics encounter within their families, and also the personality factors that influence their experience of these families. There are common developmental challenges for families, resulting in tension and asynchronous attempts at independence and acceptance.

One common clinical impression in families of women with bulimia nervosa is that they have a high incidence of sexual abuse. The research evidence exploring the incidence of bulimia nervosa is mixed, however. Some researchers think that sexual abuse is a common profile of bulimic women (for a general review of this evidence, see Ball, Kenardy and Lee 1999; for the link between child sexual abuse and bulimia nervosa, see Lacey 1990; Root 1991; Waller 1992; and for the link between adolescent sexual abuse and bulimia nervosa, see Miller 1993). Other studies (Connors and Morse 1993, a review of 11 studies) have found a percentage comparable to rates found in the overall population. Welch and Fairburn (1996) concluded that the presence of sexual abuse is a risk factor for the development of bulimia nervosa, but is not present in the majority of cases; rather it appears to be a risk factor for other psychiatric disorders in general in young women.

Pharmacological and medical effects

The physiological effects of long-term bingeing and purging can be quite marked. Perhaps the most salient physical signs associated with female bulimics are weight fluctuations and menstrual irregularities. Daily weight variations can be over 3 kilogrammes (approximately 6 or 7 pounds). Similarly, caloric intake can be variable with 25,200 kilojoules (approximately 5950 calories) being the mean daily calorific intake for women who vomit every day. Women often describe a feeling of puffiness, nausea and headaches after a binge and subsequent oedema is not unusual. Menstrual bleeding may cease due to these dramatic weight fluctuations and the undernourishment caused by frequent purging. Repeated bingeing and purging can also lead to hair loss and swollen parotid glands (the saliva glands below the ears). More serious medical complications as discussed by Goode (1985) and Lacey and Birtchnell (1985), include:

- electrolyte imbalances, primarily hypokalemic alkalosis, due to loss of potassium, hydrogen, chloride and fluid; hypokalemia may lead to cardiac arrhythmias, sometimes leading to cardiac arrest

- hypoglycemic symptoms from low blood glucose

- malnutrition-related problems including cardiovascular, renal, gastrointestinal and hematologic problems

- specific gastrointestinal difficulties including acute gastric distension and gastritis

- dehydration and fluid shifts which can lead to headaches, orthostatic (imbalance) symptoms and fainting

- insomnia

- neurological and endocrine problems

- dental or oral problems such as chronic hoarseness, painless swelling of the carotid and submandibular glands, erosion of the dental enamel and persistent gastrointestinal reflux.

Therapists need to be aware of the medical effects of bulimia nervosa not only to increase their background knowledge of the problem, but also to use as medical effects information within therapy. An account of the damage the problem can cause is often sufficiently alarming to motivate change for some clients.

Summary

Bulimia nervosa is a persistent, although not puzzling, problem in western society. The cult of the 'thin ideal' results in a culture of weight-dissatisfied young people. Personality and familial characteristics can contribute to the development of the problem. Many pass through a period of experimentation with food restriction, leading to bingeing. Some get trapped in the habit of bingeing and purging, particularly those who are passive, depressed and self-doubting. Once the habit is entrenched in the young woman's life, it exacts a heavy price. Severe medical effects for the long-term bulimic can lead to social isolation and sometimes even death.

This background information about bulimia nervosa, its occurrence and the medical implications helps us to see that the problem is common in affluent societies, and it often begins through social pressures. Knowing the behaviour is learned, however, is small compensation when it becomes entrenched in the sufferer's life. Aetiological factors become increasingly irrelevant with a problem that occurs at critical developmental stages, subsequently developing a life of its own, vicious in its dominance over self-determination.

In order to work effectively with bulimic young women, we need to understand further the above psychological, developmental and sociocultural themes. Determining whether the resultant personal tendencies are a cause or a consequence of the cycle is possibly a circular exercise for the therapist. By the time the client comes to therapy, both personal and physical tendencies are well-entrenched and bingeing and purging established as a way of life, the client requiring some assistance in breaking familiar patterns. While this chapter provided some of the evidence on the scope and significance of the problem, the following chapter introduces the themes that emerge repeatedly in the analysis of processes during therapy. The therapist's understanding of them is crucial to effective treatment.

CHAPTER TWO

Therapeutic Themes

> What pattern connects the crab to the lobster and the orchid to the primrose and all the four of them to me? (Bateson 1979b, p.16).

Bulimia nervosa is a multidimensional disorder (Gleaves, Williamson and Barker 1993) in which behavioural, interpersonal, developmental and sociocultural aspects interact to cause and maintain the problem. Accordingly, these four aspects emerge repeatedly as themes in the analysis of processes during therapy. They can be found in the client's secret, addictive behaviour (behavioural); her interactions with family members, peers, boyfriends and others, including her therapist (interpersonal); her development through the difficult passage between childhood or late adolescence and adulthood (developmental); and the social and cultural pressures on the client to be passive and to be thin, passive and feminine (sociocultural). The therapist's ability to find a path through the central issue of control that connects these themes can contribute to successful treatment of bulimia nervosa. This pathfinding is enhanced by adopting a systemic analysis of the problem. This chapter explores these themes, citing examples from clinical case studies and showing how the client's perception of control is the central issue to be negotiated in therapy.

Figure 2.1, a thematic guide to bulimia nervosa, maps the themes and is intended as a guide for both therapist and client through occasionally rough terrain. It also shows these themes clustering, in turn, around the central issue of control.

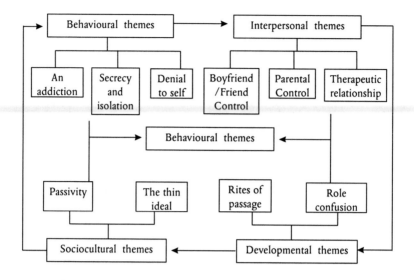

Figure 2.1 A thematic guide to bulimia nervosa

Behavioural themes involve the loss of personal control arising from the addictive behaviours of bingeing and purging, the cultivation of secrecy and isolation that develops from these behaviours and the denial of the problem to the self caused by the client's dissociated state during the behaviours. Loss of personal control over one's own behaviour is the central issue. It is ironic that women with bulimia nervosa start off trying to increase control of their lives by controlling their weight and end up by losing control of their lives to the disorder.

Moving around the guide, we come to interpersonal themes, namely difficulties with a controlling 'significant other' in the client's life. This may be a parent, friend or boyfriend who is perceived by the client as 'controlling' or attempting to control some aspect of her behaviour. Sometimes the client perceives the therapist as trying to control her, so the therapist needs to work hard to avoid this perception, simultaneously helping the client to regain control over her life. The client's lack of a sense of power in these transactions is a central issue in these difficulties.

Developmental themes arise from the way the client crosses the sometimes stormy passage between adolescence and early adulthood. She must meet the challenges characteristic of this passage, the most common being the need to establish herself as an independent person away from the controlling influence of her family of origin. Role confusion is often expressed in the client's disordered relationship to food. The challenge of independence for the client is made more difficult by the fact that the family itself is often undergoing challenges as it moves through its own developmental trajectory and that society is still rethinking women's roles in a context of tremendous change. The central developmental issue is the loss of control arising from an inability to ford transitionary periods in the client's life, her family life and her society.

Sociocultural themes emerge from cultural and social pressures imposed on the client to be thin, passive and feminine. The client's sense of self-determination plays a central role in combating these pressures. Although a sense of agency must be tempered by the awareness that there are still gender inequities in society, increasing self-determination will assist in increasing personal power and in challenging those inequities. This is particularly so for her ability to express her thoughts and emotions effectively.

All themes – behavioural, interpersonal, developmental and sociocultural – cluster around the central issue of control – that is, the perception by the client that she has the freedom to choose in the world. She often feels as although an external event or person is restraining her actions. Like a connecting band, this central issue of control runs through all these themes, presenting dilemmas for both client and therapist. The client wants to remain in the security of a delusional form of control over her life and yet she wants to regain authentic control. The therapist needs to be an active agent in reducing the negative effects of the disorder and yet he or she must not directly control the client for fear of losing her.

Behavioural themes

Bulimia nervosa has an increasing and insidious hold over the lives of many young women in terms of acquiring food, consuming it and regurgitating it. Three inter-related behaviours arise from this kind of lifestyle. The first concerns the addictive nature of the problem; the second is the secrecy and isolation engendered by the problem; and the third is the denial to the self that follows on from dissociated states of being. Each of these will be outlined below.

The addictive nature of bulimia nervosa

There are some similarities between binge-eating and alcohol or substance abuse (Watts and Ellis 1992; Wilson cited in Hawkins, Fremouw and Clement 1984). Clients often speak about bulimia nervosa in terms of 'craving', 'loss of control' and 'being hooked' and, similarly to an alcoholic or drug-dependent person, bulimics become increasingly driven by their cravings and experience post-consumptive guilt and depression. Like other forms of addiction, the effect of bulimia nervosa on a young woman's life can be financially damaging. Conversations with young women reveal that the bulimic habit is very costly. Because few women can afford the financial outlay, some resort to compulsive stealing (Pyle, Mitchell and Eckert 1981) as is the case with substance abuse. Others invent ingenious ways of camouflaging the food bills where significant others are involved in food purchasing. Just as other forms of addiction can be socially induced, there is also a contagion effect for bulimia nervosa. Conversations with bulimic women suggest that they often learn about the behaviour from friends. One woman learned about purging methods from friends. Another heard about Roman vomitoriums and decided to try the idea. Yet another read an article about gymnasts that mentioned the method and another's boyfriend teasingly suggested it after she complained about 'pigging out'. It is sobering to note how easily this behaviour can be communicated to others. Hilde Bruch (1973, p.23) states 'There is some indication that bulimia may become an intractable, chronic pattern relatively quickly and that there may be some 'contagion effect' with susceptible individuals modelling bulimic behaviours'.

The chief similarity between bulimia nervosa and alcoholism or drug dependence, however, is an increasingly poor control of one's impulses. The moments between desire and satiation grow ever more short and triggers for bingeing episodes include a host of seemingly innocent events. Often a night out is a trigger. This is where a client may deny or indulge herself. If she denies herself, she may indulge as soon as she reaches the secrecy of her home. Other stimuli to binges include stepping on the scales and finding a couple of extra kilos or simply remaining at the familiar location of gorging and purging, usually the kitchen. The late afternoons are difficult for the bulimic, particularly if she has dieted all day or had a stressful time. Some days are simply 'bad' through to the end; breakfast stretches into lunch and lunch into dinner. Discrete mealtimes become a forgotten routine.

While poor impulse control is similar in the different forms of addiction, the main difference between bulimia nervosa and alcoholism and drug dependence is the nature of the relationship to the 'trigger'. Alcoholics and drug-dependent persons can completely avoid the offending substance; bulimics have to face their demon daily when they eat and therefore avoidant strategies will not work to defeat it.

Secrecy and isolation

The second behavioural theme concerns the way in which the client must become secretive about the behaviour, isolating herself from others in order to prevent discovery of her bingeing and purging. Clients often shroud their bingeing/purging activities with secrecy in an attempt to control the discovery by significant others. This secrecy may occur in response to a fear of their own subsequent embarrassment at having others discover the way in which they manage to keep their weight down while eating. Over time, the individual cultivates a secret lifestyle around bingeing and purging, and the symptoms often go unnoticed by family and friends.

One client who had defeated the problem wrote,

(The bulimia) told me that secrecy was the only way for me and it to survive. And I guess it caused me to not only to have to keep it a secret to people on the outside but it insisted that I keep it a secret from everyone close around me and through this it imprisoned me. I couldn't reach out. I couldn't talk to people, And as time goes on, you don't trust those people. Because it becomes your best friend. It's the only thing that made me feel better... An all purpose best friend, and coping mechanism, and it also kept me trapped and kept me doubting myself and the people around me (Epston and Madigan 1995, p.9).

Women caught up in the cycle of gorging and purging often become quite ingenious at finding places and times when they can be alone. One woman living in a university residence ate a normal meal with room-mates in the communal dining hall, later collecting chocolate bars from a dispensing machine to take to the safety of her room. Occasionally, she went out looking for treats in the nearby city centre. Another teenage girl conducted midnight raids on the family kitchen, eating packets of frozen peas, raw pasta and scooping the chicken fat from the left-over evening meal.

The secrecy removes the habit from regulatory social processes such as attempts at control by family and friends. It is not surprising that women who have bulimia nervosa have few friends – so much of their time is spent concealing their bingeing and purging. Any free time can often be consumed by the weariness caused by the problem or a wariness about expanding social networks, given the problem's unpredictability. Indeed, a friend's call can coincide with a binge and lead to some awkward explanations. Intimate relationships are even more difficult. Failures are often attributed to physical appearance rather than the addictive and dishonest lifestyle that, no doubt, exacerbates normal relationship difficulties.

Ultimately, secrecy about the problem results in isolation from significant others, a gradual impoverishment of social life and a feeling of dissociation from the self. Often, the therapist is the first person to whom the client reveals the secret, sometimes after many years of the behaviour. This is an extremely difficult challenge for the client, as she must learn to let go of many forms of subterfuge in order to be helped. It is perhaps an equally difficult task for the therapist, who must acknowledge the desperation that has brought the client to reveal the secret and who must quickly establish trust and a sense of cautious hope in the therapeutic relationship.

Denial of the problem to the self

Denial of the behaviour to oneself is possibly more pernicious than hiding the behaviour from others. As noted in the model of the development of bulimia nervosa presented in Chapter One, bingeing and purging episodes are linked with dysphoria or dissociated states of consciousness. The client becomes very disoriented during a binge, the altered state often involving a loss of awareness of self and surroundings. Typically, clients experience a lack of awareness of the passage of time, the content and quantity of a binge, and the precise sequence of events leading up to the binge and occurring after it. The dissociated state also acts as a general tension reduction mechanism. Some women report a more relaxed state after a frenzied high. Others, troubled by disturbed sleep patterns and insomnia, report using bingeing as a form of sleeping pill. Dysphoria leads the client to deny to herself the true impact of the problem in her life. The client comes to minimise the problem's addictive nature and its creeping hold over many different aspects of her life. Dysphoria and the associated denial to the self results in the behaviour becoming more entrenched over time. One of the chief obstacles to therapeutic progress will be the client's ability to become aware of the circumstances, content and internal state provoked by the bingeing and purging.

In summary, women with bulimia nervosa lose control over the behaviour of bingeing and purging and deny to the self and others the effects of this loss of control. Loss of control over these behaviours means that women generally feel that that they are out of control and increasingly distant from others, family, friends and work or school colleagues. If the behaviours continue unchecked, their social networks quickly become restricted and impoverished.

Interpersonal themes

Besides losing behavioural control, clients are often 'out of control' in significant relationships. They struggle with parents who unsuccessfully try to control them, and with boyfriends and friends who misguidedly attempt to help them. They sometimes even feel powerless in therapy and experience their therapists as too directive. The client's sense of her own power in relationships is the final interpersonal theme to be discussed in this section.

Struggles with parental control

Bingeing and purging can quickly reduce the sufferer's sense of her own power or personal agency and this, in turn, is reflected in 'control struggles' in her relationships with others. During therapy, the client often speaks of a parent who is 'controlling', or showing some controlling behaviour, in relation to his or her daughter's problem. One client described her mother as 'superachieving' and her father as 'controlling'. Mother had been off and on diets most of her life and was so attuned to the regulation of her own weight that she could look at any photo of herself and know exactly what she weighed. She often used food as a reward for the children's good behaviour. Father was 'very self-controlled' – he was obsessive about fitness and tried to control his family's access to the kitchen. He loathed the children standing in front of the fridge with the door open, worrying that they would make the fridge 'ice over'.

It is the client's perception that parents try to control her well into adulthood. One mother, understandably alarmed by her daughter's problem, attempted to regulate her daughter's bulimic symptoms by questioning her after she suspected her daughter had been bingeing and vomiting. Unfortunately, given the client's sensitivity to issues of control, this attempted solution exacerbated the problem and a related problem grew up about the control or ownership of the bulimia. If the daughter perceived that mother was questioning too much, she increased the frequency of bingeing and vomiting.

Struggles with control: boyfriends and friends

Similar unintended consequences have resulted in response to 'over-involvement' by boyfriends or friends. When one client's boyfriend took it upon himself to rebuke his girlfriend whenever he thought she had binged, she responded by deliberately defying his rebuke with another and often more severe binge. At the same time, he was attempting to reduce his alcohol intake and responded to this covert message of defiance with an alcoholic binge. Unfortunately, both people in this interaction, although well-intentioned, increased their addictive behaviour in response to each other's misguided helpfulness. The attempted solution only exacerbated the difficulties and another problem arose, constituting ownership of the original problem. Open defiance of the other's emotional incursion was never entertained, the need for compliance being too strong to allow the expression of outright anger or even disapproval.

Friends' dress codes and behaviours provide an even less direct, but equally as strong, form of control. Often clients will completely subjugate their own standards in deference to their friends, rather than balance their own with others' standards. One client's sense of control over her acceptability and desirability was given over to others as she compared herself to their unexpressed standards and found herself wanting. She was acutely aware of her peers' mocking eyes. This was an 'outside in' perspective that played itself out in strict adherence to norms about dress codes, acceptable weight levels and physical appearance. The client's perception of these eyes made them seem like fun-parlour mirrors distorting and magnifying her body. Yet another client compared herself physically, emotionally and professionally to others, often feeling envious of their achievements or physical appearance. She focused exclusively on others' achievements to the extent that she lost sight of her own achievements and sense of direction.

Control and the therapeutic relationship

If control presents as a contentious issue in relationships with family, friends and lovers, it follows that it will also present as a central theme in the therapist–client relationship. The client's attempts to control the relationship are indirect yet powerful, often inversely proportional to the degree of her awareness of them. There are many examples of these attempts within therapy. She often and unconsciously attempts to control the conversational stream by indirect and frustrating (for the therapist) methods. Questions are ignored and topics inexplicably changed. Tasks, even though suggested by the client, are conveniently forgotten by the following session. The therapeutic hour often comes and goes with the client forgetting or arriving late yet again. If the therapist in a weaker moment accepts the invited position of all-powerful expert, the client will work hard to relieve her of this role as quickly as she has been elevated. Even the client's own suggestions are countered with that persistent and elusive game of 'yes-but'. Clients also think they are not in control of the therapeutic process – they often feel they do not have any choices, no matter how client-centred an approach the therapist may adopt. It is almost as if client and therapist are in the therapeutic process to fulfil some pre-arranged plans that have pre-ordained outcomes, none of which are of the client's construction.

The client often senses that she is either in control in a relationship or that the other person is in control of her. Therapy might be the first relationship where neither of these alternatives is a possibility. It then becomes a hard struggle for the client to begin to let go of her need to control or be controlled so that change can actually begin. Once the client knows she can determine the process, she often takes a far more active role in the choice of subject to be discussed. One client said she was not aware she had an option until I asked if she felt she could make time in the sessions to talk about something of significance to her. Until that time, she did not realise she could define the parameters of our discussion.

The client's power

Similarly to the way in which they are unaware of their own presence and influence in the therapeutic session, many clients are not aware of their own power in general transactions. How can they be when they are so emotionally invisible? So much of their time is spent searching for clues from the therapist as to their own worthiness that they are blind to their own input. Pleasing the therapist is intricately woven with the client's inability to know the effect she has on others. Pleasing the therapist becomes a damaging game because the relationship is prevented from deepening to a more authentic level.

This keen observation of others accompanied by her lack of assertiveness is evident across all interpersonal domains, family, lovers, friends and even the therapist. Awareness and expression of her own desires and needs is one of the chief ways in which the client can break some of the unhelpful patterns that develop with parents, friends and boyfriends. The therapist must also work hard to avoid manipulative struggles with the client, even although the client may be completely unaware of them. Both the following and the final chapters of this book will explore some of the ways in which the therapist can work with the client, not against her, to increase her awareness of her own presence and impact in personal relationships. The following section leaves the interpersonal theme to explore another common therapeutic theme, those critical transitions in life through which clients try to pass and in which they often become stuck.

Developmental themes

According to the developmental perspective, the adolescent's ability to negotiate critical transitory periods in her life will predict her level of risk for various problems (Attie and Brooks-Gunn 1992). Two critical periods for the adolescent are first, the passage into adolescence and second, the passage out of adolescence into young adulthood. During the passage into adolescence, the child must integrate her changing body into her self-image; loosen ties to her parents and move towards greater autonomy; develop sexual relationships with others; and internalise a value system independent of her parents. During the later transitionary period, the young woman must establish intimacy in relationships, pursue an education and a career, and develop an identity apart from the family. The core struggle in all areas is the establishment of an independent identity despite considerable confusion about her role. In the following sections, I describe the nature of the struggle for bulimic women in therapy as they move from dependence to independence, emphasising clients' often expressed confusion about on the roles available to them. I close these sections by speculating on the way in which critical life transitions can reflect family life transitions and those of the larger societal milieu.

Rites of passage: from dependence to independence

From a developmental perspective, the passage into adolescence and then into early adulthood marks transitionary periods in life. The critical issue in both is the ambivalence that the young person feels about dependence on and independence from her family of origin. Many clients want to remain within the safety and support of the family and yet they know they need to take risks outside the family in order to become adult. One client's pivotal dilemma, her ambivalence about moving from dependence to independence in her family of origin, invoked notions of perceived powerlessness. She did, and did not, want to leave her mother. Leaving would have signalled her emergence as a female adult with all the responsibilities and risks that this involves. Also, she identified with the perceived powerlessness of her mother and she did not like this. She wanted to do more than move outside the orbit of her mother – she wanted to move outside the domestic way in which her mother had played out her female role. This thought often led to shaky and nervous feelings and shifting ground where the client realised she must construct her own rules outside those of her family and her society. The way in which this theme interplays with the larger societal theme of women's development is reflected in the often difficult relationships between mothers and daughters.

The sometimes ambivalent feelings that mothers have towards their daughters compound the tensions experienced in this relationship. The daughter's independence often signals the rejection of the mother's role – the daughter rejects the mother's nurturing role and simultaneously reproaches her mother for inadequate nurturing. Some feminists argue that the mother's conflict can express itself in inadequate emotional feeding of the daughter. Eating, as a response, becomes the way for the daughter to express the many conflicting aspects of the conundrum that is their relationship.

Fathers are also very important for their daughters' development. Fathers who are absent, either physically or emotionally, impinge on a girl's sense of herself and her psychic conflicts are played out with one parent alone, with all the knotted density that this concentration invokes. Feminists argue that we should be wary of the 'mother-bashing' and 'father coddling' that abounds in the clinical literature (see Luepnitz 1988 for a discussion of this literature). From a systemic perspective, the father's contribution, even if absent, must be taken into account as a considerable factor in assisting the young woman to make the transition smoothly and effectively from dependence to independence.

The family itself is also in transition, moving from one developmental stage to another as the parents redefine their purposes in life and the nature of their marital relationship and their relationships with their children. Often parents of women in therapy are just beginning to understand that they need to relinquish their control of their children. Often, too, adolescent crises can interact painfully with parents' mid-life crises, with their questioning about quality of life issues. Sometimes, the adolescent with bulimia nervosa will be co-opted (unwittingly for all parties) by her increasingly distant or hostile parents into providing a reason for temporary marital union or cohesion. It is not uncommon to hear that a parental marriage is disintegrating just as the client is improving.

That the bulimic member might serve some cohesive purpose in a family in distress is not a reason to pathologise the family as dysfunctional, however. The use of crisis to cause the family to rally is well within the limits of normality. It is also an established principle that people will rally against some common cause. That the symptom has been produced by the daughter to unite the marriage has yet to be proved, and until such time, citing the family as the cause, no matter in how subtle a way, is unnecessary for improvement and may inadvertently trigger a perception by the family that it is 'enmeshed' and hostile to the client's interests. Family members, however, do need to know the ways in which their behaviours are contributing to the continuation of the problem and need to change them if necessary.

Role confusion expressed through food

The core struggle in the period ranging from late adolescence to early adulthood is the establishment of an identity. My clients are pressured to make occupational choices, to compete in the job market or at university and to become financially independent. They are also asked to commit themselves physically and emotionally to intimate relationships. These are difficult challenges in themselves, but exceedingly more difficult when they are placed in a context of the very short history of women's emancipation. As a consequence, young women are often unsure about society's expectations of them.

In developmental crises, young women look to their mothers to provide a model of identity and are forced to turn away, confused and ambivalent about the role of nurturing portrayed by their mothers, and the role of achieving demanded by a growing section of society. Given women's traditional role in preparing and regulating food intake, it is not surprising that food becomes the arena in which this confusion plays itself out. Unfortunately for some, the confusion becomes a vortex into which the young woman slips, forever repeating the same ritualistic taking in and casting out, moving forwards and moving back, risk-taking and scuttling for the safety of old ways.

As more and more time is taken up with the consumption and elimination of food, important life choices may be shelved. Indeed, it is not unusual to hear clients speak about food and weight regulation as if it were a career. Achievement is epitomised by the attainment of a target weight. The cyclic episodes of stuffing and purging polarise her days between the domination of 'the good self', (that is self-denying, nurturing others, self-absent) and 'the greedy self', (that is, full of self, self-indulgent). Achievement is epitomised by a day of being 'good', of going without, and stands in sharp relief to 'bad' days of gluttony. This form of achievement with its association with Victorian morality seems a treadmill, the client aspiring to greater and greater success, the horizon forever retreating. Certainly the problem has critical educational and career implications for young women in addition to marked personal and social costs.

It is ironic that the cyclic episodes of stuffing and purging provide a sense of order and purpose in the client's life, so much so that the prospect of the existential vacuum left by a 'cure' is frightening, and is often enough to send the client scuttling back to the safety of the problem's predictable patterns. One client found the absence of the polaric tensions of cyclic episodes of stuffing and purging in her cure profoundly disturbing, as if the future was a great void, empty of purpose. Food was the engine that sent her hurtling by the same carriage down the same circuit for many years, and the ritualistic grooves, once abandoned, left her stranded at an existential way-station, bereft of meaning. Authenticity – being true to herself and realising the full potential within her – demanded that she let go of rigid ways of being. It asked her to pay the price of this by facing the subsequent anxiety, terrifying though it was.

Bugental (1990) suggests that in a very real sense the client must go out of control for at least a brief period because the ways in which control has previously depended have been bound up with old patterns of being. Until they are truly let go, they cannot be replaced.

The developmental themes found in therapy with women with bulimia nervosa are characterised often by the denial, avoidance or displacement of authentic life choices. Through her symptoms, the client denies or avoids the shift from dependence to independence in her family of origin or becomes entangled in the family's need to shift from one developmental stage to another. Decisions about intimate relationships and career choices are displaced by her obsession with food. In order to improve, she needs successfully to address the challenges of increasing independence and establish adult and assertive relationships with family and loved ones. Her focus must increasingly shift to those challenges typical of her life stage, the establishment of a career and, if she so chooses, an intimate relationship.

Sociocultural themes

> Femininity, in essence, is a romantic sentiment, a nostalgic tradition of imposed limitations. Even as it hurries forward in the 1980's, putting on lipstick and high heels to appear well-dressed, it trips on the ruffled petticoats and hoopskirts of an era gone by (Brownmiller 1986, p.2).

Sociocultural themes emerge, either directly or indirectly, at different points of treatment for clients in therapy, but often towards the latter stages. There are two main sociocultural themes. The first theme includes societal prescriptions about how much women should weigh and how they should look, particularly how they should conform to the notion of femininity. The second theme concerns the direct expression of a woman's needs and emotions, especially her anger. Both themes are explained below.

The 'thin ideal' versus the real

The first theme involves the prescription about the 'thin ideal' that predominantly comes from the media. Despite an intellectual awareness of the damaging effects of these images on their self-image, my clients invariably feel inadequate about their weight and want to be thinner. Each perceives herself through the eyes of a critical phantom onlooker and finds herself wanting.

She does not seem to know herself from the *inside out*, from the sense of unique rightness about one's body that is the lot of children – but rather from the outside in, from critical eyes that stretch endlessly onwards as in a long hall of mirrors (Orbach 1986). Because she has an *outside in* perspective, she is an ardent watcher of others, so that the slightest nuance – an expression on the face, a movement of the hands – is confirmation or rejection by the other. Her self is validated by what others think she should be and feel.

This perceived and often critical gaze puts this facet of the theme as an extension of male appropriation of the female form where a woman had to learn to regard her body as a commodity, an item to secure a viable economic future. Although societal conditions have changed, some feminists argue that a woman's present position in life still shows lingering traces of its precariousness. Since the core of her being is built around pleasing others, she is faced with the sometimes impossible task of making her body into whatever is currently acceptable. John Berger's analysis, although written in 1972, still has validity for today

> A woman… is continually accompanied by her own image of herself… she has to survey everything she is and everything she does because how she appears to others, and ultimately how she appears to men, is of crucial importance for what is normally thought of as the success in her life. Men act and women appear. Men look at women. Women watch themselves being looked at. This determines not only most relations between men and women but also the relation of women to themselves (Berger 1972, pp.46–4).

This struggle to close the gap between the ideal and the real represents another facet of the central issue of control, one that can block effective treatment in that it discourages self-determination and opts for comparison and rejection. There are many reasons to spurn the 'thin ideal' and to encourage self-determination. Social practices that construct women in distinct categories by lumping them into 'the ideal' or 'the unattractive' constitute an external logic, one that converts an average difference into a categorical difference (Connell 1987). The homogenising effect of the 'thin ideal' disregards the tremendous degree of difference in the human form. The 'thin ideal' acts as a mesmerising agent blinding us to these differences, a tight box of a category that does not open out to life but closes, constricts and denies. The 'thin ideal' is an *outside in* perspective – a curious one given the different historical and geographical constructions of the human form.

The therapist needs to encourage clients to notice and accept the wide variability in the female form. It is worthwhile here to examine other times and places when different fashions prevailed. As Brownmiller (1986) comments, Botticelli's Venus is slender enough by today's standards but Tintoretto's Susannah, or the harem women in the Turkish Bath by Ingres, while de rigeur in their day, are gargantuan by comparison. The therapist can also point out male appreciation for this wide variability, although caution will need to be exercised because some women, for various reasons in their personal histories, are ambivalent about, or even fear, male attention.

Passivity and getting angry: 'the good and the greedy'

Passivity is the second and most salient of the sociocultural themes. Many clients depict themselves as passive observers of their own lives as opposed to active agents. For example, one client, a student, would not consider asking a lecturer for guidance, would not speak up in tutorials for fear of saying the wrong thing, and befriended her boyfriend's friends rather than pursuing friends of her own. If one views this theme from an individual perspective, repeated feelings of being out of control with food predict a reactive stance and a feeling of being ineffective in the world.

From a psychological perspective, however, theorists (Duker and Slade 1988; Orbach 1986; Wolf 1990, 1993) claim that passivity is not surprising given the marginalisation of women's experience. They argue that passivity is reinforced by an ascetic and female cultural tradition of denying her own wants in order to nurture others. In therapy, many clients are unable to express their own wants and needs. They seem to be unconsciously steeped in this self-effacing heritage. If they can control such 'bad' desirous feelings, they are protected by a mantle of moral 'good'. The therapist's task is to help the client uncover intrinsic desires, thoughts and feelings and to use them as guides to her place in the world. Validation of one's feelings and emotions is perhaps the core of a sense of effectiveness in the world.

Associated with the client's passivity is her inability to express emotions directly, particularly anger. In the first instance, clients seem to be confused about the difference between emotional 'hunger' and physiological hunger and will often 'eat over emotional feelings' rather than 'talk the feelings up'. It is interesting to note that early in therapy, I often ask my clients to distinguish between hungry feelings and emotional feelings; and many report back the following session saying they were simply hungry from food restriction.

Others will use food to handle strong emotion. If clients perceive they have committed emotional sins by demanding too much, or asking for redress for a slight by another, then food becomes a vehicle for handling the often turbulent emotions that ensue. One client, after a scene where her father threw her belongings out of the door and in response she demanded respect, quelled her strong feelings with a binge. Another, after being told of her incompetence at work, came home to comfort and punish herself with an excessive intake of food and a lengthy bout of bingeing.

Even if clear about the nature of the feelings they experience, clients often feel that their emotional needs are of less importance than their boyfriends', friends' or family members' emotional needs, that they are less entitled to the attention and validation of others. Anger then is a rare emotion for these women.

> Anger in a woman isn't 'nice'. A woman who seethes with anger is 'unattractive'. An angry woman is hard, mean and nasty; she is unreliable, unprettily out of control. Her face contorts into unpleasant lines: the jaw juts, the eyes are narrowed, the teeth are bared. Anger is a violent snarl and a hostile threat, a declaration of

war. The endless forbearance demanded of women, described as the feminine virtue of patience, prohibits an angry response (Brownmiller 1986, p.163).

For women trained in this tradition, the immediate response to disappointment and hurt is to feel hopeless and helpless and to continue in the feminine tradition of compliance and agreeability. These observations accord with Orbach (1986) who writes, 'In woman after woman, I have observed a pattern in which needs and initiations are ignored, disparaged or thwarted in some way' (p.140).

Like Orbach's clients, my clients feel they need to control their own responses in order to answer the needs of others. For example, one client felt that she must not 'speak up' about her boyfriend's continual lateness; she felt that she did not have a right to express her anger, indeed, that she did not have a right even to feel angry let alone request a change of behaviour. Her confusion in the initial sessions with me centred on what she called 'inappropriate emotions': her response to her boyfriend's lateness was that her emotion, her anger, was inappropriate. Her role, as she perceived it, was to be emotionally invisible, to control, and occasionally obliterate, her expression of feeling. Unfortunately, this response to strong feeling also obliterates a sense of self, since a sense of entitlement to feelings and emotions is the gateway to personal preference and the definition of oneself in the world.

Sociocultural themes concerning the 'thin ideal' and the client's passivity, even although they may appear later in therapy, are no less important to address in assisting with the problem. The client's inner sense of who she would like to be in the world needs to be promoted above the tyranny of the 'thin ideal'. Equally needed is encouragement of the client's direct and constructive expression of emotion, even anger, even though this may be very frightening for the client.

Summary

We have seen that four major themes emerge in the analysis of processes during therapy. These themes concern the client's addictive behaviour (behavioural); her interactions with family members, peers, boyfriends and her therapist (interpersonal); her development through the difficult passage between childhood or late adolescence and early adulthood (developmental); and the social and cultural pressures on the client to be thin, passive and feminine (sociocultural). The following two chapters explore the ways in which these themes can be addressed during therapy. The next chapter, Chapter Three, shows the general systemic procedure to be used throughout the stages of treatment. The following chapter, Chapter Four, shows useful tasks for addressing each dimension of the problem – behavioural, interpersonal, developmental and sociocultural. Chapter Five shows the general procedure for use in each individual session.

Stages of Treatment

Some people don't ask you what would be helpful. They make
assumptions about that and don't acknowledge you. This makes
you want to fight them more (eating disorder group member
quoted in Kraner and Ingram 1997, p.44).

Overview of the stages

This chapter shows the overall stages of systemic treatment for
bulimia nervosa. The sequence of themes presented in Chapter Two –
from behavioural, interpersonal, developmental to sociocultural – is a
useful way to approach the multiple facets of bulimia nervosa in
therapy. This sequencing of the themes can be used to structure the
flow of sessions across the course of therapy. The sequence is depicted
as a flow diagram. The first stage is information gathering followed
by stages which focus, in turn, on behavioural, interpersonal, developmental and sociocultural themes. The final stage is termination and
relapse prevention (see Figure 3.1).

The first stage is preparatory. Information is gathered on the
background and significance of the problem in the client's life. In the
second stage, she attempts to change the repetitive behavioural
patterns associated with the problem. The focus of the third stage is
on interpersonal problems that the client is currently experiencing,
with some focus on the past. In the fourth stage, the client addresses
developmental challenges as she moves from dependence to independence. The fifth stage focuses on the sociocultural aspect of the

problem, the role of women and notions of femininity. The sixth and final stage addresses termination of therapy and the prevention of relapse by the client.

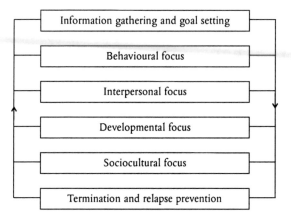

Figure 3.1 Stages of treatment for bulimia nervosa

The use of a simple flow diagram with returning arrows to depict the sequence of stages is intended as a general guide for structuring the flow of events across the course of therapy from the first stage through to the fifth stage. The returning arrows suggest some degree of flexibility within the sequencing, and the possibility of a return to former stages to revisit insights, reinforce new habits or, indeed, explore another aspect of that stage altogether. Some stages may not be emphasised because the client's needs will be different and client progress seldom proceeds sequentially, smoothly and evenly through the stages. Treatment needs to build flexibly on each woman's unique set of circumstances rather than on models and prescriptions (Kraner and Ingram 1997). The main point is to be aware of the general pro-gression of stages, so that all themes are covered.

In this chapter, I will outline the aims, objections and general principles and concepts for covering each of the stages. In the following chapter, I show the specific tasks and interventions to be used within and between each stage, each designed to address specific themes of the problem.

Stage one: information gathering and goal setting

This stage typically comprises one session, of one-and-a-half to two hours'duration, the purpose of which is to introduce the client to the approach, to gather general background information on the impact of the problem in the client's life and to establish goals for treatment.

Introduction to the approach

The therapist needs to introduce him or herself, to give qualifications and experience and to describe the general way of working (including for example, adherence to session times, frequency of sessions and payment). Particular attention should be given to explaining the purpose of the tasks and interventions to be used to break the habit of bingeing and purging and to gaining agreement to trial these between sessions. The therapist should explain that reporting back on the outcome of tasks attempted between sessions will form the basis of the initial part of the next session. The approach and evidence on the approach should then be presented to the client and compared with other treatments.

Information gathering

Background information is then collected. This is a critical stage in therapy because both therapist and client gain a comprehensive understanding of the nature of the problem, so that false starts in addressing it may be avoided. Addressing most areas will help the therapist avoid neglecting potentially important data. Collecting comprehensive information is particularly important for those who are beginning to work in this area because it helps to avoid both therapist and client bias (Nezu and Nezu 1993). Not all information will be important, of course, but it is useful to touch on each specific area so that a comprehensive picture of the problem is obtained.

It is crucial to take time to explore fully first the precipitating event that has brought the client to therapy, and second the background and history to the problem. Some of the information can be collected in the form of psychometric instruments (surveys and questionnaires – see Appendix for a review of the most relevant). These could be mailed to the client after the initial contact with the therapist. The client could answer them prior to commencing therapy and the data obtained would provide the basis for discussion during the initial session. I often ask the client to fill out a depression inventory, a self-esteem questionnaire and an eating disorders questionnaire. While psychometric information of this sort provides an excellent basis for discussion, there should be a strong sense that therapist and client are co-constructing the impact of the problem over time, rather than that the therapist is 'investigating' the problem and that the standardised data is the only valid source of information.

A broad-based exploration of possible difficulties that the client is experiencing across a variety of areas could include:

- information about the frequency and severity of bingeing and vomiting (this is gained by asking the client during the intake telephone conversation to keep a record of the frequency, form, severity and duration of binges and purges in the preceding week and the week leading up to the session – see Chapter Four)

- the history of the problem, particularly dieting and weight dissatisfaction (sexual abuse might be able to be discussed but the therapist should be extremely sensitive to any discomfort the client feels here)

- the history of attempting to reduce the problem. An inventory of what has worked and not worked gives useful guidelines for devising tasks and interventions in therapy. Knowledge of how the client experienced previous professionals may also help the therapist shape the treatment plan. If the client was upset by prior treatment, it is important to find out why and to modify your approach if this seems necessary

- how the client is generally feeling about life, her internal conflicts, particularly her levels of depression and possibly suicidal behaviour

- the quality of her interpersonal relationships (marital, family, parent–child, friends, work or school contacts)

- her career, job and school history

- her physical health, physical symptoms, use of drugs and leisure. Without alarming the client, some attempt should be made here to inform her about the medical effects of the problem and the fact that a little weight (approximately 2 kilogrammes or 5 pounds) is gained usually from treatment – this motivates change

- her personal goal attainment and resolution of life choices.

During this first session, clients should know that they are free to terminate at any point. I typically suggest that they call me after this session to tell me of their decision to proceed so that they do not feel caught in therapy with a therapist with whom they have little rapport or confidence. I also let clients know of others who work in the field and of their general approach so that they can pursue treatment with another clinician who is more *simpatico.*

Goal setting

Another important purpose of this first session is to establish challenging but achievable goals. Setting specific, measurable, and achievable goals is one of the most important therapeutic interventions. Although set in the initial session, they may be revisited at any stage later on. The focus here is on how the client is contributing to a solution to the problem rather than how she is maintaining the problem. It focuses on what is possible for the client rather than how she is limited by the problem. Strategies for helping the client determine her goals are found in the next chapter which is on tasks and interventions for each stage of therapy. One important principle for helping the client to determine her goals is to encourage her to frame the goal positively. A negative goal, such as 'not bingeing and purging', will keep the client focused on the cessation of bingeing and purging rather than what she wants to have happen in its stead. I typically will not leave a goal unless I have helped the client to frame it positively, and in measurable terms. There are a number of excellent therapeutic strategies for this explained in the next chapter.

Externalising the problem

It is also important in this session to begin to externalise the problem, that is, through language to pit the person against the problem. The therapist needs to separate the person from the problem and thereby to counteract the 'totalising' and pathologising effect of the problem. This also helps the client to feel more powerful in relation to the problem and if she can feel more powerful, she will begin to feel more hopeful. Then, therapist and client can work together against the problem. I will often use a 'fighting' metaphor to describe the client's experience: for example 'You were fighting it, so it decided to sneak back up on you'. Externalising questions can be used throughout the information gathering and data collection phase. For example, in gathering information about the history of the problem, the therapist could ask such questions as:

- What do you remember in your life that most helped bulimia along?

- Did the suffering you were going through somehow assist in bulimia's getting a grip on you?

- Has the media message of 'thinner is better' pulled your thoughts away from noticing other qualities about yourself?

- Can you remember qualities of yourself prior to bulimia's onset that you would like to keep alive and nurture?

- Can you remember qualities of yourself prior to bulimia's onset that you would like your family and friends to remember?

Stage two: behavioural focus

The main aim of this stage of treatment is to normalise eating behaviour and to reduce the frequency and severity of bingeing and purging. The objectives are: to encourage a climate of experimentation rather than success or failure in defeating the symptoms; to identify different types of hunger (for example, mouth hunger, boredom hunger, stomach hunger) and the means to satisfy the type; to establish discrete meal times; to incorporate taboo foods into the diet; to reduce dieting and weighing behaviour; and to encourage a wider social network and less secretive behaviour concerning the bingeing and purging.

The strategies for achieving each of these objectives are described in Chapter Four. Here it is important to outline the main principles behind these strategies. The principles are ongoing record-keeping, restraining change, impulse control and social regulation.

Record-keeping

It is important to continue to keep records as they will provide good information for how to proceed. Records of an event, including what was eaten, any feelings or thoughts during the crisis, and the circumstances leading up to the event and after the event can be analysed for unhelpful patterns. An example of such a form is found in Figure 3.2.

Sample record of bulimic episodes

The event	Quantity eaten	Feelings	Thoughts	Events preceeding	Events following

Figure 3.2: Sample record of episodes of bingeing and purging

Restraining change

It is also important to invite the client to restrain change at the beginning of treatment in order to encourage her to observe her own behaviour. This will not only help to provide further valuable information but also help to avoid the therapist becoming entangled in dilemmas about who has ownership of the problem. It is likely that a reduction in the symptoms will occur as a result of this 'don't change' prescription. The rationale behind paradoxical strategies such as these is that if a symptom, is by definition beyond control then the client is exercising control by choosing to have the symptom. A number of other paradoxical interventions will be mentioned in Chapter Four.

Impulse control and normalising eating behaviour

Experimentation with delay and substitution strategies can also be utilised at this stage to good effect. Impulse control is the chief ally of behavioural restraint; therefore determining the efficacy of different strategies for different conditions is critical to improvement. Unlike other addictions, the client must have contact with the addictive substance in order to live, therefore she must find out how to delay or substitute the gratification that comes from the bingeing or purging behaviour. She must also learn to reward herself for progress, first by noticing that she has made progress and second, by immediately reinforcing constructive behaviour with activities she would find normally pleasurable. While the frequency of bingeing and purging is being reduced, the therapist can begin to help the client return to normal eating patterns by reducing triggers, such as weighing, and encouraging healthy eating habits, such as instituting discrete and regular mealtimes, including 'taboo' foods in the diet, and identifying and satisfying the different types of hunger.

Social regulation

The client should be encouraged, under the guidance of the therapist, to begin to disclose the behaviour to trusted family and friends and medical professionals. Often clients are concerned about the effects of long-term use of bingeing and purging on their health. A visit to an understanding doctor will be necessary to allay fears or realistically appraise damage. The doctor should be chosen wisely as some have been known to shame their clients, believing that the problem was somehow a moral failing. If the behaviour is subject to social regulation and 'feeds on secrecy', then she needs to break this stranglehold by disclosure to trusted informed friends, family and medical personnel and by deliberately cultivating a wider social network.

Stage three: interpersonal focus

The main aim of this stage of therapy is to identify and resolve problems in interactions with significant others. The objectives are: to facilitate awareness of needs, desires and motivations and intentions; to encourage directness in communication, particularly the constructive and assertive expression of anger and hostility; and to encourage others to support change in a positive direction. The main means of achieving these aims and objectives is to conduct an 'interpersonal inventory'. The actual involvement by significant others within the therapy could also be indicated, particularly where client progress is slow or at a standstill.

The interpersonal inventory

The interpersonal inventory of problematic relationships gathered in stage one should be expanded here (Klerman et al. 1984). Crucial relationships, both past and current, need to be reviewed in order to determine the nature of the interaction with significant others. Gather information about each person who is important to the client, including information about the frequency of contact, activities shared and so on. Help the client to determine the satisfactory and unsatisfactory parts of the relationship, whether their expectations are fulfilled in the relationship and whether the significant other is also fulfilled. Assist the client to articulate the kinds of changes she wants in the relationship, whether this comes about through changing her own behaviour or bringing about changes in the other's behaviour. It is a good idea, after a thorough examination of significant relationships, to identify repetitive patterns in relationships, the problem areas and some personal goals that the client wants to achieve in relationships generally. One challenging avenue for exploration of interpersonal relationships is to discuss openly the positive and negative feelings between the therapist and the client and to seek parallels in other relationships.

Challenging rigid patterns of thinking

Clients' rigid patterns of thinking often contribute to difficulties in interpersonal relationships. Black and white thinking, over-generalisation and all-or-nothing thinking can distort the client's perception of her role in conflict situations. It is important to show ways in which the client can surmount these self-defeating patterns. The client should be encouraged to notice disturbing emotions she experiences in relationships and to name the thoughts that precede these emotions. Self-defeating thoughts can then be named and challenged before they gather momentum. The client can be assisted to name and then challenge destructive thought patterns, first in the analysis of processes in therapy, and second in the tasks between sessions.

Therapeutic involvement by significant others

Sometimes it will be necessary to involve others in the client's therapy. The usual indicators for inviting others are slow or no progress or interpersonal difficulties that are ongoing and that could threaten the client's progress. In a situation of little progress, there is often another who has an unconscious but vested interest in the status quo. In therapy, they can be assisted by the client and others who are involved to see the impact of their actions. The client's full permission is needed to involve others as she could find this situation very threatening. The therapist needs to maintain a neutral and balancing manner in group interviews with couples, or family or friends of the client. The therapist is both an advocate for the client and sympathetic and respectful of the group's hierarchies, norms and mores. The main method for encouraging the group to support the client's progress is to encourage the free circulation of information. This should be information about the client's and others' goals, perceptions, feelings, and attitudes typically in relation to the client's symptoms, or critical group incidents. Circular questioning is a useful therapeutic strategy to encourage this kind of sharing (see Chapter Five for an explanation of this strategy).

Stage four: developmental focus

The main aim of this stage of treatment is to help the client develop life-goals and to resolve satisfactorily the challenges of each life-stage. In order to do this she will need to become more clear about her own values, dreams and aspirations and she will need knowledge of the typical challenges of each life-stage for both the individual and for the family (if this is relevant to her situation). The chief means for achieving these ends are information about life-stages, life-goal clarification, skills inventories and career guidance and metaphor and rituals to symbolise transitions. The important point to remember here is that the desire to move on in life will be a natural outcome of satisfactory progress in defeating the problem. It will not need to be introduced artificially by the therapist, but rather encouraged and nurtured when the motivation to develop, no matter how small, appears in therapy.

Information about life-stages

The client can be helped to list the various passages and transitions she has made in her life and to examine the resources she had to make those transitions successfully. She can also be assisted to see that the family itself has life-stages, the tasks of which need to be addressed successfully in order to move from one stage to the next.

Life-goal clarification

There are a number of exercises for clarifying values and goals found in the following chapter in the section on developmental tasks and interventions. Some clients will find it relatively easy to list their values and goals; others who have been entrenched in the problem find it more difficult. The therapist needs to choose the type of exercise (from structured to unstructured) to suit the temperament and point of development of the client.

Skills inventories and career guidance

If it is appropriate, I help the client to determine her skills, after helping her to identify her goals. The gap between her current situation and desired state will then be clear and she can begin to determine what she needs to do to achieve her goals. I tend to avoid defining goals in terms of specific positions, but focus on values more. A broad value orientation allows the client to feel fulfilled by a number of different positions within the context of life circumstance and constraint. Of course, specific information about different vocations should be offered by appropriate professionals.

Metaphor and rituals to symbolise transitions

Sometimes rituals can be used to signify a transitionary period. Letting go of the past or destructive patterns or persons can be symbolised in objects or acts. Some transitions are straightforward and direct and others are indirect, making use of metaphor, ritual and symbolism. Choosing the type of exercise to help the client will depend on her general orientation and personality. I often use the metaphors that clients use in therapy as avenues to suggest a ritual that may be useful. Some of these will be suggested in the next chapter.

Stage five: sociocultural focus

In this stage, the aim is to encourage the client to consider how social and cultural factors have helped to shape the eating disorder. The culture's emphasis on the 'thin ideal', weight dissatisfaction and dieting need to be analysed from the personal perspective. Specific objectives of this stage are to raise awareness of societal depictions of femininity, particularly the motives of the fashion industry; to discourage self-surveillance not based on objective data; to hold the culture accountable, if necessary, for inducing unrealistic body goals and expectations; and to take back ownership and enjoyment of how one appears to others. The chief means of achieving these aims and objectives is by observation, discussion and encouragement of new ways of viewing familiar circumstances.

It takes time and psychological space to understand the ways in which the culture has influenced her personal choice in dress, behaviour and aspirations. Reflection also needs clarity of thought, an open mind and tolerance of the outcome of the thought process. The Zen saying that self-knowledge is insulting can be applied here to the realisation of the motives that make women vulnerable to the fashion industry. It is a painful to realise how much one has been duped by status-seeking into destructive fashion habits.

I believe that the main way to achieve insight in this area is to relate the client's personal experience to historical, cross-cultural and ethnographic perpectives on femininity, gender roles and eating disorders. Relating personal experience to the wider social context will usually arise quite naturally during the latter stage of therapy, often not in an anticipated way. I sometimes use a client's insight about the personal aspects of her life as a platform for discussion of the general social or political issues. For example, one client told me about her boyfriends; the discussion then drifted to their actions so we could examine the implications for fairness and principle in their actions and her reactions, contrasting the norms for behaviour in our culture with other cultures. Another client was hurt by comments about her appearance in her workplace, as she strove to conform to workplace standards. A simple comparison of the rules in her work culture with rules in other work cultures was enough to prompt the realisation that her colleagues' opinions were idiosyncratic to that workplace and outmoded. The client did not need to change but needed rather either to work within the culture to change it, either directly by remaining within the culture as a 'loyal oppositionist' and making formal complaints through legitimate channels, or to change it indirectly by supporting others with more liberal viewpoints into positions of influence. Regardless of the approach, the therapist is a facilitator of the client's realisation of her own opinions and should not assume the role of didactic teacher.

The use of groupwork is an important method for exposing clients to alternative ideas about women's role in society. Other members of the group in similar predicaments should give the spectrum of views on women from conservative to radical and encourage her to pursue her own views. Despite some preliminary evidence to suggest that groupwork is useful in the early stages of treatment (Hamilton 1999), I think the potential for entrenching destructive thinking and demoralisation is too great and would not use groupwork until the latter stages of therapy. The indicators for groupwork are, at the minimum, resolution of the major behavioural aspects of the problem, the need for a broader social network or an impasse between therapist and client.

Stage six: termination and relapse prevention

When clients have reached their goals, it is important to leave enough time at the closing of the session to deal with termination. Both client and therapist typically decide when goals have been achieved although other decision criteria should be used, such as client self-report, feedback from significant others, and the therapist's own observation. It is critical at this point to help the client summarise all that she has learnt and to suggest that relapse might occur: 'It may be that, during a difficult time in the future, you will find yourself being drawn back by the problem. Let's sort through how you are going to gather your resources to turn away from the problem again.'

The research evidence suggests that relapse is likely if there is a greater frequency and severity of initial symptoms or negative affect, such as depression or low self-esteem (Stice 1999). Predicting a temporary relapse can help cushion the inevitable angst that the client must go through in order to find a more solid sense of self. I often predict that a stressful circumstance might be marked by confusion and can be accompanied by a brief return to the former bulimic behaviour. I 'normalise' this relapse, if it does occur, by saying that it is acceptable given the radical change in direction. A clear distinction should be drawn, however, between recurrence (that is, occasional over-eating which is normal) and relapse (a full return of the bingeing and purging). Specific constructive actions and thoughts during therapy should be reviewed and then therapist and client should develop a relapse or contingency plan. Relapse plans will show early warning signs and the specific actions and thoughts useful during therapy to fight the problem. The client should rehearse coping with high-risk situations.

Metaphors that describe the process of recovery as a search for new meaning, the very beginning of the journey, and that allow a period of confusion while the client finds her feet are useful. One effective image is that of the client clinging to a lifeboat after a shipwreck. In this metaphor the client decides to abandon the lifeboat and swim to shore. Just when she is the most tired and very close to shore, she must battle huge waves that might sweep her back out to sea. The final struggle finds her at the shore disoriented and exhausted, needing to rest and to ready herself for the beginning of the journey.

It is also important to explore the client's arrangements for continuing support. The therapist will be encouraging an increase in the range and depth of social contacts throughout therapy so that by termination, the client should be able to name at least five close contacts she can turn to in difficulties. The client should also be made aware of others in the professional community to whom she could turn if the therapist is not available.

Attempting to resolve the client's and your own feelings about parting can be difficult, but crucial to authenticity. You model very real ways of dealing with high and sometimes painful emotions if you are honest about how you feel. The client will learn effective ways of dealing with sad feelings by watching you.

This chapter has posited six stages of treatment, ranging from the information-gathering initial session to a focus on the behavioural, interpersonal, developmental and sociocultural aspects and then the termination process and relapse prevention. The six stages are not intended to be undertaken in a lock-step fashion but are capable of differing emphases given the individual differences and needs of clients. For this reason, they are thought of as a flow diagram with potential to revisit former stages, depending on the client's individual needs. The following chapter provides specific tasks and interventions designed to address the four themes discussed in Chapter Two. Behavioural, interpersonal, developmental and sociocultural tasks and interventions will be outlined, showing the way in which they should be used to assist the client.

CHAPTER FOUR

Effective Tasks and Interventions

Specific tasks and interventions drawn from the four themes that emerge during therapy should be used when treating bulimia nervosa. This chapter outlines these tasks and interventions for behavioural, interpersonal, developmental and sociocultural aspects of the problem. I will show the considerations that need to be used in selecting tasks and interventions, the general progression through the thematic areas, and the tasks and interventions that I have commonly used under each of the four thematic areas.

Considerations for selecting tasks and interventions

An intervention is an event or series of events typically devised and introduced by the therapist for the purpose of reducing destructive symptoms or developing some aspect of the client's cognitive, behavioural or social life. A task is an exercise, ideally co-constructed by therapist and client from material that has occurred within the session, to be undertaken by the client between one session and the next. As such, a task is a specific type of intervention with far greater input from the client.

There are several considerations when selecting a task or intervention. First, it is important to achieve a fit between the identified problem and the broader context of that problem – for example, a behavioural problem requires a behavioural solution and similarly, a developmental challenge requires an intervention or task addressing the developmental nature of the problem. Second, the task or intervention generally should arise out of the client's concerns expressed during the session. Preferably these will be co-constructed with the client; however, in the first few sessions, this is often difficult for the client and the therapist will probably initiate and structure the tasks and interventions. Third, all therapeutic contact should emphasise the positive and use the client's and the system's strengths as levers for change. Given the level of demoralisation and defeat for most clients, acknowledging and emphasising strengths is crucial for success. Fourth, interventions should be designed to promote assertive behaviour. As noted in the chapter on therapeutic themes (Chapter Two), clients are often extremely passive and need to be encouraged to express their needs and desires. Often this will initially swing into anger but, where possible, assertive behaviour should be encouraged.

Fifth, tasks and interventions should be focused on the present and action-oriented, targeting specific problems. Once again, this helps to fight against the long-term despair that has usually surfaced once the client comes to therapy. Sixth, interventions should target sequences of behaviour within and between multiple systems that maintain the identified problem; the greater the systemic coverage, the better the chance of effectiveness. Finally, where possible, interventions should be designed to promote long-term change across multiple systemic contexts.

General progress across the thematic areas

Interventions may occur at any time but tasks need to be addressed by the client predominantly between sessions. Tasks have far more chance of being successful if they are based on the ways in which the client has been successful in the past, avoiding those that were unsuccessful and linking in with the client's goals. One of the first goals of the initial session with the client is to establish effective and ineffective strategies that the client has tried. Weakland (1990) proposed the axiom 'if it works, don't fix it; if it doesn't work, do something different'. This is a simple axiom which is often ignored when selecting tasks, and yet it is so important to effectiveness.

The following four sections show various tasks and interventions across the four thematic areas: behavioural, interpersonal, developmental and sociocultural. Tasks will be posed at the end of the session as 'homework' for the next session and much of the initial part of this session will be spent discussing the client's response to them. Interventions will typically be conducted during the session. They are presented in the sequence in which I often use them.

Behavioural tasks and interventions

Encourage an attitude of experimentation

Rather than assessing the client's response to tasks as 'pass' or 'fail', encourage clients to view their efforts to reduce the bulimic behaviour as experiments, and to consider themselves as experimenters receiving valuable feedback about their efforts to reduce the behaviour.

The reactive effects of record-keeping

A useful first session task is to ask the client to keep a diary of bingeing or purging during the ensuing week. In a sense, this is a paradoxical task because you are asking the client not to change so that you can observe the pattern of bingeing and vomiting. The reactive effects of record-keeping are well noted in the behaviourist literature – the very act of observing and noting frequencies, places, emotions and thoughts preceding and subsequent to the binge-purge episode often decreases the behaviour's occurrence.

Identify the type of hunger

Ask the client to identify the type of hunger they experience and then to respond to it with an appropriate action. The following suggestions for different categories, adapted from Orbach's book, *Fat is a Feminist Issue* (1978), can be used, although the client might want to construct her own. Social hunger will mean that meal times are important because people can be together. Mouth hunger will mean that the client wants to put something in her mouth, although she does not feel hungry in her stomach. Prophylactic hunger is anticipatory eating because in a couple of hours when she cannot eat she will be hungry. Deserved hunger is cheering yourself up with food because you have had a bad day. Pleasure hunger is eating something because it is one way she knows how to give herself pleasure. Nervous hunger is eating something because it controls her anxiety. Celebratory hunger is eating because it is the only way she knows how to enjoy an occasion. Boredom hunger is making a sandwich because she cannot think what else to do. The client can also rename the hunger in terms of what can satisfy it and then take action to satisfy it; for example, if the client is celebrating with food, she may like to experiment with treating herself to a movie. If she is eating because she had a bad day, she can comfort herself with a warm bath.

Establish that dieting leads to bingeing

There is a growing body of research to suggest a causal link between dieting and bingeing so it is sometimes useful to show the client these journal articles (e.g. Hart and Chiovari 1998; Huon 1994; Polivy and Herman 1985). One client found that this was a breakthrough – once she saw the literature she decided to stop dieting. The client should also be assured that only modest weight gain should occur as a result of therapy. Since large quantities of calories are consumed during a binge, with a sizeable portion being retained even when the client purges, the overall number of calories or kilojoules consumed by the client who eats regularly without bingeing is usually the same as or even less than the number of calories or kilojoules consumed when eating irregularly and bingeing (Spangler 1999).

Establish three meals a day

Encourage the client gradually to introduce three meals a day with in-between snacks. We should not forget how radical a departure from the norm this behaviour is, so a gradual introduction is best. Instituting breakfast is a good first step and later, if the client feels able, two meals a day, then three. The important point here is that the meal is discrete – that it has a distinct beginning and end. Ignore the continuation of bingeing during this phase. A useful metaphor is that the client is repairing the structural components of a building. The old life will eventually and naturally become irrelevant once the stronger new structures are in place.

Do something different

Encourage the client to 'do something different' the next time she feels like a binge. Usually this takes the form of a delay or substitution strategy, such as 'walk in the garden', 'phone a friend', 'have a bath', 'play your favourite music' or 'play with the cat or dog or children'. The client either delays the binge or physically cannot binge at the same time as she is undertaking the activity. One cannot eat while talking on the telephone. If the client decides to binge, then she must go through the same strategies before purging.

There are a number of ways in which the client can vary the behaviour if she is bereft of ideas for the former task (some of these are paradoxical and therefore need to be used with care as to their timing and impact):

- change the location of the problem – for example, the client should binge and vomit in the hallway or bedroom if she usually does it in the kitchen

- change who is involved in the problem – for example, ask father to prepare the evening meal if mother usually does it

- change the order of the steps involved – for example, purge before bingeing

- add a new step or complaint to the problem – for example, go ahead and binge but listen to relaxing music before you do so

- increase the duration of the pattern – for example, binge for longer and purge for longer

- introduce arbitrary starting and stopping – for example, tell yourself you will have a binge at three o'clock and finish at four o'clock

- increase the frequency of the pattern – for example, have more frequent binges that last a shorter time

Incorporate a taboo food

Encourage an 'and-also' approach to food by asking the client to incorporate into her diet a food she has hitherto rejected as taboo. Severe restriction of the variety of foods only invites excess. If the client can experiment with different foods while she is in control, they will not be a trigger to out-of-control eating.

Normalise the link between eating and social discourse

Offer to conduct a counselling session over lunch. This can be very difficult for the client but the positive benefits are numerous – she trusts you and will follow your lead. You model a discrete beginning and end to the meal, eat slowly and show that sharing a meal with someone you like can be pleasant. You break the stranglehold of secrecy that accompanies eating behaviour. You can talk about how normal it is for the stomach to distend with food and how this should not be taken as a sign of over-eating (which is often a cue for a binge).

Discourage weighing in

Promote the gradual decrease in the number of times the client weighs herself as this is also a common cue for bingeing and purging. Establish a baseline frequency at the beginning of counselling and promote the rewarding of a decrease with a favourite activity (not eating!).

Paradoxical tasks

If the client is not responding to direct attempts to reduce the frequency of bingeing and purging, indirect and paradoxical tasks may be useful. Paradoxical tasks mainly are symptom prescriptions, that is, 'don't change' prescriptions that are often accompanied by the client's keeping a diary of what she ate and how she felt when bingeing. There are many variants of symptom prescription: asking the client to maintain the prevailing rate of bingeing and purging so that the pattern can be observed; asking the client to plan a binge and to carry it out with a list of prescribed food, or to have a spontaneous binge when she does not feel like it; issuing a dictum to 'go slow' accompanied by a suggestion to return briefly to bingeing for study purposes – the point of the communication being that the client is controlling the rate of bingeing and that a return to bingeing could happen and is part of getting better. The logic here is that the client is asked to try the very thing that she feels she has no control over. If the client does not change then she can be congratulated for not changing, the implication being that she is in control. After trying these tasks clients often report that they did not make it through their carefully arranged list; they wondered what it was about bingeing that intrigued them so much in the first place. Sometimes the thought of deliberately choosing to have the binge or purge is enough to avert a binge-purge episode for the client without necessarily carrying out the behaviour.

Other methods may be adopted if the above strategies do not have the desired effect. Vognsen (1985) proposed either an ordeal if the client was 'co-operative', or a challenge if the client was 'resistant'. The ordeal was that the client must wake herself at 3AM on the days when she had binged, the ostensible purpose being to get at 'stubborn sub-conscious motivations'. If the client was resistant, the client was to involve herself more directly – for example, the therapist may question the possibility of improvement, that the client is not able to 'tolerate the pleasures of being normal' or the therapist may refuse to give any more homework assignments since 'the client does not seem ready to try them out'. I find these strategies distasteful!

Good days and bad days in relation to food

Many clients divide their days into 'good' and 'bad' depending on their ability to restrict food or their ability to go without bingeing.

Rather than have the client polarise her days, it is good to encourage her to begin to classify these days along a continuum from one to ten. A continuum has the advantage of implying movement or progression and challenges an 'either-or' approach to food.

Break the stranglehold of secrecy

Because bulimia 'feeds on secrecy', the client is asked to tell someone she trusts – this will 'starve' the problem. This should be a trusted friend or family member. I usually also ask the client to break the secrecy by a visit to the doctor. This must be a doctor who is sympathetic and knowledgeable about the problem. Some treat the problem as a personal and moral failing, rather than a clinical disorder. A visit to a medical practitioner should address health fears about the long-term effects on the client's health.

Set specific, measurable and achievable goals

Goals are identified through positive outcome questions, for example, 'How will you know when the problem is solved?' or 'How will you know when things are going better for you?' (rather than 'What is your problem?'). Variants of this type of question include the miracle question – 'If a miracle happened overnight while you were asleep and tomorrow morning you found yourself free from the symptoms, happy, satisfied with your life, what would be happening differently?' – and the video question – 'If I had two videos of you, one where the problem was gone and one where you had the problem, what would I be noticing about the one without the problem? What would I notice that is different about you in that one?'. These sorts of questions are often followed by 'first sign' or 'first step' questions; for example, 'What will be the first sign that this goal has been achieved?' or 'What will be the first step towards this goal?' (see Table 4.1). It is important to note here that all questions use language that assume that change is not only possible, it is inevitable. The structure of the question 'How will you know…?' invites the client to look out for indicators that the wished-for goal has been achieved.

Table 4.1: Goal construction questions

Client goals are encouraged through the use of solution focused and future oriented questions. For example, 'How will you know when thing are going better?' or 'How are you going to know, when you have gone without vomiting three, four or five times, that it is no fluke?' These questions imply that change is inevitable, that is, it is not a question of whether it is going to happen but when! De Shazer (1982) claims that the latter question also defines the achievement of the goal, that is, that three, four or five times means the problem is solved.

Goal construction questions may take the form of:

miracle questions for example, 'If a miracle were to happen tonight while you were asleep and tomorrow morning you awoke to find that this problem was no longer a part of your life, what would be different?'

video descriptions questions for example, 'If we had two videotapes, one of you in the past when the bulimia nervosa was really on top and the other some time in the near future when things are better – what is more noticeable about the tape of you in the future that will tell us that things are better for you?'

small step questions for example, 'What will be a small sign – something that you will notice in the next week or so – that tells you that things are going better for you?'

scaling questions for example, 'On a scale from one to ten, with one being very bad and ten being quite good, where would you rate how you are doing now?' and 'When you're able to say [the number the client wishes to be] what will be happening differently?'

Goals may also take the form of doing something different.

De Shazer (1985) proposes that unique reactions provide the basis for solutions; therefore, clients are often advised to do something different from what they ordinarily do in relation to the problem. In relationships, 'doing something different' changes the complementary or symmetrical nature of difficult problems. A variation of this task is 'Pay attention to what you do when you overcome the urge to binge', which implies that the client has already done something different.

Interpersonal tasks and interventions

Facilitate awareness of needs, desires and emotions

The client can keep some sort of record of her needs, desires and emotional life. This may be by means of a journal, poetry or artwork. This will validate the emotion, find words to express it, and allow the release of strong emotion. Simple exercises suggested in the section on behavioural tasks and interventions can be expanded into longer writing tasks exploring underlying feelings and thoughts – for example, recording the types of hunger suggested in the previous section can grow to include an exploration of past times when the client has felt this hunger, typical ways she has satisfied the hunger and creative ways she may satisfy it in the future.

Use mirrors

Some clients have found that they increase awareness of their own presence in eating behaviour and normal social discourse if they place mirrors in strategic places around their home. They gain consciousness of their actions and information about how they might appear to others.

Use tapes of the session

With the client's permission, I sometimes record the session and invite her to take the tape and replay it at her own convenience. She can be asked to note critical points in the transaction, or her own interpersonal skills. Better still, if client and therapist review the tape together, they can elaborate on particular points during the discussion, expressing what was unsaid, or identifying useful or not useful patterns in the interaction.

Assist the client to express strong emotion constructively

I interpret a client's swing from a passive, unaware state to a very angry state as the first sign she is getting better. However, these needs have to be expressed constructively so that damage is not done to significant relationships. The expression of needs can be used to assist clients to develop more authentic relationships. Needs are usually examined in the context of a critical incident that has been presented during therapy, and the client will then explore the circumstances surrounding the incident – what happened, what were her thoughts, feelings, and behaviours, the triggering event, what she would like to do more or less of in the future. She may ultimately need to modify her expectations about the relationship or the discussion may pinpoint faulty communication in dealing with the problem. Whatever the outcome of the discussion, the relationship should be shown to be related to the eating problems and the client should consider and be shown ways of becoming real with others.

Encourage the client to be assertive

When conflict occurs in a relationship, encourage the client to review the dispute and identify the issues and differences in expectations and values. Both client and therapist can then identify options and resources to bring about changes in the relationship. It is important to examine conflict closely. Are there parallels in other relationships? What is the client gaining from the conflict? What unspoken assumptions are linked to the client's behaviour? How is the conflict perpetuated?

Teach assertiveness and conflict resolution skills

It may be necessary to teach ways and means of being assertive in relationships, identifying needs rather than wants, and expressing these in terms of 'I' language which describes rather than accuses or avoids the offending behaviour. Some clients will need to undertake consciously speaking up for their own need as a disciplined practice in their relationships.

Teach the client to type and counteract destructive thought patterns

Encourage the client to categorise her upsetting thoughts according to the typology offered by cognitive-behavioural therapy. Women with bulimia nervosa often have a number of beliefs (documented by Root, Fallon and Friedrich 1986, p.117) that need to be challenged.

These beliefs are often the root cause of her part in difficult interpersonal relationships. They may include:

1. I must be approved by everyone for everything I do

2. I should be in control and competent at all times

3. If things do not go as I have planned, I am out of control

4. If people really knew me, they would think I was a terribly weak and uninteresting person

5. I should be able to satisfy all my needs

6. I should be productive at all times

7. I am responsible for everyone's feelings

8. I should be considerate at all times

9. If anything goes wrong, it is my fault.

These need to be categorised according to black and white thinking, all-or-nothing thinking, over-generalisation and so on and a countering statement made. For example, counter statement 1 (all-or-nothing thinking) with 'I cannot possibly be approved by everyone for everything I do. If I was, I would begin to lose all sense of myself and cease to be a person. I can learn to live with choosing when to please those who are important to me and forgetting the rest.' Countering these kinds of thoughts needs to be practised assiduously because, according to behavioural theory, the client will inadvertently reinforce destructive thoughts if she does not challenge each and every one. The unwanted thoughts might grow stronger as a result. This warning needs to be given if and when she chooses to eradicate destructive thoughts.

Declare your impotence if you do not know what to do next

Sometimes therapist and client reach an impasse. No matter what the therapist tries, the client has tried it and it has not worked or she does not think it will work if she tried it. A useful but seemingly manipulative intervention proposed by Selvini-Palazzoli *et al.* (1978) is for therapists to declare their impotence by saying they are defeated by the problem and do not know how to proceed. Often the client's response is to offer other ways of proceeding and the deadlock is passed. I have declared my impotence when I literally have exhausted the repertoire of my interventions. The impasse has been broken but, despite my genuine intent, I am left with a lingering feeling of duping the client. No doubt helping professionals must come to terms with their ability to manipulate, control, persuade and influence through the use of particular skills. I have partially resolved this dilemma by thinking it is for the good of the client. Still, the doubts remain!

Reduce client isolation

Wherever possible, the client should be encouraged to reach out to others and to form new relationships. A clear link should be made between increasing social isolation and the progression of the eating disorder. Linkages should also be made between well-being and a wide social network.

Developmental tasks and interventions

Alleviate stress

Where the binge-purge cycle seems to be fuelled by stress, then some of the best remedies are very simple and easily found in the client's life – taking the time for leisure activities, rest and recreation, exercising regularly and getting enough sleep. Prioritising the day's tasks into 'must do', 'nice to do' or 'don't do' will help to cope with great demands. Watching or playing sport seems to be a strong protective factor for young women and girls. Therefore the client should be encouraged to engage in some sporting activity whether for pleasure or competition.

Clarify life values

Encouraging the pursuit of values helps set the client up for success, whereas encouraging the pursuit of certain positions or jobs may set the client up for failure and distress and perhaps a return to the bulimic pattern. A broad value orientation allows the perception of satisfaction in many different positions. For example, I encouraged a client who had set her goal as a certain senior position with the government to discover the values underlying that particular position. For her, these were to make a contribution to society, to have financial success and to receive acknowledgement from others for what she did. Many positions could have fitted this broad value description and she gradually opened out to different potentialities and possible sources of career satisfaction. This is an 'and-also' approach to life rather than the characteristic bulimic 'either-or' approach; the latter unfortunately restricts possibilities.

Identify life goals

Sometimes the client is so locked into the problem, she does not know how to begin to formulate her goals. One task I have given that seems to be successful for people who do not have any idea of career or life goals is to draw up a sheet of paper with three column headings: 'To be', 'To do' and 'To have'. In each column the client writes things she would like to be, to do and to have. She generates as many possibilities as she can, allowing herself to be as crazy, silly or imaginative as she would like to be. At the end of 20 minutes or so, she circles three to five goals that would be challenging, but not impossible for her. These then become the basis for determining long- and short-term goals.

Conduct a skills inventory

Once the client is clearer about where she would like to go in her selection of a career or in the identification of the next step in her career, ask her to conduct a skills audit. Ask her to identify the skills she has and the current workplace opportunities. Then she should identify the skills she needs and the skills 'gap', those skills she needs to gain in order to fill the gap between her current and desired state. Both therapist and client then construct an action list for how to gain these skills.

Use metaphors to evoke readiness

The concept of 'readiness' is invoked particularly when clients feel they are not on top of the bulimic behaviour. I often use a 'life raft metaphor' to evoke readiness, suggesting that when the client is ready she will let go of the life raft and swim to shore. This is useful because it suggests difficulties to be addressed in metaphorical and easily understood language; for example, breakers near the shore will try to pull the client under when she is tired after a long swim. It is precisely at this time that she should not give up or interpret the fall (relapse) as a failure, but rather summon all strength and keep moving on. Also, of course, the metaphor suggests that reaching the shore was the beginning of the journey 'on solid ground'.

Encourage the client to move through transition periods

If the client is moving between one role and another, for example, from adolescence to adulthood, and feels stuck and unable to make the transition, encourage her to review the positive and negative aspects of old and new roles and to explore feelings about what is lost. Discussion on opportunities in the new role as well as the change itself will be useful. Therapy should assist the client to develop a social support system and new skills called for in the new role. The therapist needs to help the client develop a sense of mastery regarding the demands of the new role. It is helpful if all experiences during this time can be framed as 'learning' rather than 'successes and failures'.

Use rituals to symbolise and encourage movement through transitions

Sometimes transitions can be best captured in rituals. The client can mourn the loss of an old role by participating in a ritual. One client who spoke of a river of resentment about the injustices in her childhood gathered symbolic objects representing her childhood and floated them down a stream near her home. Another wrote a farewell letter to her old role and an invitation to her new role. Whatever the mechanism for making the transition, the therapist needs to assist the client to regard the new role as more positive.

Invite an audience to a new self-description

When clients have taken significant steps to 'win' over the bulimic behaviour, if they so desire, then others (partners, family and friends) can be invited to a celebration. In effect significant others can become, where appropriate, an audience to a new self-definition. This is most important when the problem is nested firmly within interconnected interpersonal spheres. Significant others in the client's life can be brought together to mark the beginning of a new and more hopeful stage for the client. If significant others are not encouraged in this way to acknowledge the client's progress, they may inadvertently continue in behaviours that invite the client to relapse. While simple celebrations are usually very useful, sometimes tying such celebrations to rituals that the group finds significant can be even more powerful. Often clues to the sort of appropriate celebrations can be found in the metaphors that the client and/or significant others use in therapy. For example, one client continually referred to flushing away parts of herself. Once the family was alerted to improvement, they came together to witness her flushing symbolic objects representing the problem down the toilet. Burning, burying or partying can all be effective given the needs of the client and the particular family.

Sociocultural tasks and interventions

Discourage passivity and encourage choice

Casting light on the fine-grained aspects of choosing and deciding in terms of the client's emotional life is one of the first tasks of therapy. The exercise of effective choice is the first affirmation of self, where a woman gives to her own experience the currency she offers to the experiences of friends, family and lovers. Following are some of the ways in which the client can begin to exercise choice and thus combat passivity. These should emerge from the day-to-day decisions she currently needs to make. However, within therapy, she could be encouraged to construct goals for her own life, to choose tasks she will perform between sessions and to control the rate of therapeutic progress. Ask her to experiment with making one decision a day and then to observe how it went.

Encourage direct emotional expression

Control or abuse of food intake are often attempts to cope with emotional upset. The client should be encouraged to 'feed all the different emotional needs she feels' rather than 'stuff or dull down the emotions with food' or 'talk the feelings up rather than eat over them'. It is common to find that a woman who is getting better will begin to feel very angry. Feelings of anger towards another can be usefully reframed as a positive sign, an affirmation that the client is getting better. Ways of expressing dissatisfaction to others without getting the other offside are provided by the principles and practices of assertiveness training and conflict resolution. Clients often benefit from awareness of 'I' and 'detoxified' messages.

Invite discussion about societal depictions of femininity

Direct challenges to societal norms of the 'thin ideal' are likely to be met by an equally intense or frightened defence of them. This is particularly true for the late adolescent age grouping (even when the client intellectually understands their damaging effects). The presentation of dilemmas, however, allows the client to realise that she can choose whether she wants to live more of a life for herself or more of a life according to others' ideas of who she should be! Dilemmas are two-sided descriptions that reflect the client's ambivalence about change, although the language selected by the therapist is often biased towards one of the options. 'Should you move forward to a life where you are independent and trying out new and risky things or should you mark time in a more dependent life, one where you need others' approval before you can try a new behaviour and where you must always look to others to get what you need?' Such a question presents two possible future developmental pathways, highlighting one as preferred.

Encourage awareness of shapes and fashions over the ages

Encourage the client to view the varying fashions and changing shapes over the ages and between cultures. View art books depicting the human form and how the ideal has changed down through the ages. Both client and therapist should look beneath the surface of such variations to discover their meaning.

Encourage dressing to please the self

Ask the client to take one day where she deliberately dresses the way she would like to rather than the way she perceives others would want her to dress. This may be to wear more make-up or no make-up, to look outrageous or demure or to wear clothes that do not match. The point is to soften her rigid approach to clothes, style and dress.

Reinstate family or social meals

Take action to reinstate family meals so that parents can model good food choices and eating behaviour becomes subject to interpersonal regulation. If parents have poor choice in food, then the client can help steer her family towards a better diet by shopping and cooking for them.

Create supportive environments

There is a social contagion effect for dieting and binge-eating, so high body esteem and healthy eating habits need to be encouraged in the school system through educational and peer support programmes. The client may wish to become involved in such programmes.

Encourage social action

If the client so wishes she can be helped to press the government for tighter regulation of the fashion and beauty industries. Increasingly, children are portrayed in advertisements and fashion and product campaigns. Related industries are also targeting children as consumers. There is much to be done to regulate some of these consumer practices: boycotting magazines and products that promote distorted images of women, writing letters to magazines explaining why you have chosen to boycott, and lobbying politicians to regulate the images we see in our magazines.

The client may also wish to join a group in order to make some changes. An example of one such group is the Vancouver Anti-anorexic Anti-bulimic League (Madigan 1994). It enables group members to transform from 'patients' to community activists and consultants. It is a grass-roots organisation with regular meetings, a newsletter, and specific membership committees. Its aim is to help the community become conscious of practices that objectify women's bodies. The Media Watch Committee, based in Vancouver, denounces pro-bulimic activities against women such as department stores' use of waif-figured mannequins or gymnasium advertising designed to induce guilt. The School Action Committee, also based in Vancouver has developed an anti-anorexic, anti-bulimic programme for primary and secondary school students. The point is that in helping at the level of community, young women can assist other women, and in turn, help themselves.

Participation in community development projects will enable therapists and clients to establish linkages with key people within the community who can, in turn, educate others. One such project, the 'House of Mirrors', was sponsored by the Association for Awareness and Networking around Disordered Eating (ANAD), another Vancouver group. This was a visual arts installation of 26 full-length mirrors on to which women and artists portrayed the impact that the media, diet, fashion and cosmetic surgery industry have had on their lives. A 'House of Mirrors' typically contains flaws in the glass, causing the reflections they cast to be distorted. This was seen to be an appropriate metaphor for the distorted images reflected back to women every day. Several community people were specifically selected as representatives of particular groups (bankers, business groups, the fashion industry) to sponsor and promote the project, ensuring that assumptions are debated in areas not normally associated with such debate.

Use the metaphor of Jeremy Bentham's The Panopticon

There are similarities between the way the client surveys her body and the design of prison architecture so that prisoners can be constantly and centrally surveyed. One of the most influential designs for prisons of the nineteenth century, The Panopticon, by the philosopher Jeremy Bentham, is a useful metaphor for the client to encourage her to see the way in which she imprisons herself by constantly surveying her own behaviour. The design of Bentham's prison was based on a perimeter building in the form of a ring. At the centre of the perimeter building is a watchtower with windows opening on to the inner face of the perimeter. The outer building is divided into cells with one window to the outside allowing daylight to pass through the whole cell and another window facing on to the inner part of the perimeter. The overseer in the central tower can then pick out, from the back lighting, the captive silhouettes in the ring of cells.

Foucault (1984) uses the metaphor as an example of how the medical gaze (similar to the penal gaze) was institutionalised in a system of centralised observation making bodies visible in space. He comments that the overseer in the watchtower can capture the inmate (whether a lunatic, convict, patient, worker or schoolboy) far more effectively than if the inmate was held in a dungeon, the darkness affording a kind of protection (pp.146–147).

The metaphor can be used to explore how the client came to be a prisoner, how others may have become overseers, and how the client is now both overseer in the watchtower and inmate in the prison cell. More importantly therapist and client can explore the opportunities for escape from the prison, and discuss how she will avoid returning again.

This chapter has summarised the main tasks and interventions that I have found useful in the treatment of women with bulimia nervosa. The conditions for choosing tasks and interventions have been listed and they have also been categorised according to their focus – behavioural, interpersonal, developmental, sociocultural. The following chapter shows the general procedure for the conduct of each session.

CHAPTER FIVE

General Session Procedure

This chapter summarises the general session procedure to be used within each session. It is intended as a general guide only, showing the way in which I usually structure each session. The procedure is predominantly derived from the strategic and systemic approaches and therefore uses many of the practices of those schools (see Boscolo 1991; Boscolo *et al.* 1994; Brown 1994, 1997, 1999; de Shazer 1982, 1985; Furlong and Lipp 1994; Haley 1976; Madanes 1981; Madigan 1994; Moley 1983; O'Connor 1984; Selvini-Palazzoli *et al.* 1978; Turnell and Lipchik 1999; Watzlawick, Weakland and Fisch 1974; White 1986a, 1989, 1990, 1991). Before outlining each step of the procedure in order, I emphasise the value of questions which are the main way of achieving the objectives of each of step the procedure.

The value of questions

In accordance with the tradition of the schools mentioned above, questions are the predominant form of the therapeutic approach in each session. Circular questions in particular are used. These are questions that help clients draw connections and distinctions between information, thereby tracing patterns in experience. They also invite the client to control the process and content of the session. Gregory Bateson (1979b) thought that all learning occurred by means of double description, that is, placing disparate information together so that one could contrast and compare. An analogy here is that learning is similar to the difference between monocular and binocular vision. Monocular vision is one-eyed and flat; binocular vision gives the added bonus of depth perception. Questions need to be structured to invite multiple descriptions of events, that is, the client should draw connections and distinctions between one category and another and see the same event or situation from different perspectives. This viewing of difference can happen along any of the dimensions specified in the thematic analysis of bulimia nervosa – behavioural, interpersonal, developmental and socio-cultural.

The therapist can ask questions that notice differences:

- over time – when did the problem begin? When is it most difficult?

- between people – who between the two of you shows the most involvement with the problem?

- between parts of a person – are you ruled more by your feelings or your thoughts when you binge?

- between situations – are you more likely to have control over the purging in private or in public?

Alternatively, the therapist can encourage the client to see connections through questions. Connections can be drawn between:

- behaviour – when you both agree, does it bring you closer together or push you further apart?

- feelings – when you think she is watching you, what feelings do you have?

- beliefs – when you think there is danger in expressing your anger, do you think that brings you closer, or separates you?

- meanings – when your mother said she rejected you, how do you think she got that idea?

- relationships – when he says he is coming and does not do so, how do you think that affects the relationship?

Circular questions are used throughout the procedure. The following section summarises this procedure through each session.

Socialising

General conversation sometimes helps the client feel at ease, particularly in the initial sessions. I use the same language as the client to 'join' or build rapport. However, I do not linger in general conversation too long; a few minutes suffice to settle in the client and help her to feel she is in a friendly place.

Record-keeping

Responses to tasks, in addition to the collection of information about bingeing and purging, will be included in this first part of the interview. Record-keeping helps the therapist to remember important aspects of the sessions. A record of responses to the tasks that the client attempts during therapy to decrease the bulimia will help in devising further tasks and interventions to defeat the problem. Often the first part of the session will be spent discussing the information gained from record-keeping.

It is important to encourage the client to notice small wins with the problem. Often women who have had bulimia for a long time will be blind to their own progress, not noticing that they are making strides towards their goals. The therapist needs to be vigilant, continually reminding clients about progress they have made since the last and very first session. Therapists can reinforce change in the desired direction by asking clients how they have managed to make such changes in the time between sessions. A number of clients have told me that they were despairing of reaching their goals when they walked into the office and much more hopeful and resourceful when they walked out because I thought they had made progress, no matter how small. Incremental progress may not be observed without careful record-keeping.

Problem statement

The problem statement is the client's response to the question 'What would it be useful for us to talk about today?'. The client then usually gives her account of the problem or associated problems and therapist and client pursue this as a topic of discussion. If the client does not know what she wants to talk about, circular questions are used, for example, 'If your (boyfriend, mother, friend) were here, what would they advise us to talk about?'. Clients are often unaccustomed to choosing the topics and will often flounder if asked these questions directly. Asking for a topic from another's perspective often helps to stir fixed ways of looking at situations. If the family or part of the family is involved, it is important to ask about each person's ideas about the problem in order to contrast and compare different perceptions about the problem: for example 'Who is most concerned about the problem?' or 'What does your brother think about the problem?'.

Relative influence questions

This is an important motivational stage of the interview where the client understands the full effect of the problem in her life. This is done by mapping the effect of the problem, that is, understanding the influence of the problem in the life of the client – for example, 'In what ways has the bulimia been a problem for you?'. The second stage, helping her to see that she does have some personal agency in the problem, is to map the influence of the client in the life of the problem ('In what ways have you got on top of the bulimia?'). This approach to questioning is again based on externalising the problem, that is, through language, locating the problem outside the person, and then pitting the person against the problem. The description of the problem is usually drawn from the way in which the client describes the problem during the interview. There are many examples of externalising using relative influence questions – 'In what ways has bulimia affected your relationship with yourself?'; 'In what ways has your relationship with yourself stood up to the influence bulimia wanted to have on your life?'; 'By what means did bulimia get you into isolation and despair?'; and 'In what ways have you managed to remain hopeful in spite of bulimia's negativity?'

Complementary description

Questions are then asked that encourage two-sided and circular description of events. Clients are often confused about the linear relationship between aspects of the problem. They are unsure, for example, whether bingeing leads to the vomiting or vomiting leads to the bingeing. They become confused, not understanding the circular nature of the problem. Clients can be encouraged to entertain circular descriptions of events, that is, to consider how the bingeing leads to vomiting and then the vomiting leads to bingeing. The therapist can advise that isolating a single cause is not necessary because the client can start anywhere in the circular chain of events and can make a change. For example, if she is not sure if she binges because she feels tired or she feels tired because she binges, I often pose the problem as a circular 'vicious circle' and encourage an 'and-also' way of thinking about the problem. This allows solutions to be found at any point of the 'vicious circle' as opposed to finding causes to the problem. Interpersonal circularity can sometimes be difficult to understand for the client and her significant others. The client should be asked to consider mutual interaction around the problem: for example, 'How does your not speaking about the problem encourage your mother to ask you lots of questions?'. Then you might ask the mother, 'How does your asking questions when your daughter gets home from school encourage her to keep the problem a secret from you?' or 'How does your stepping back from the problem invite your mother to step forwards and claim the problem as her own?' followed by 'How does your stepping forwards to claim the problem invite your daughter to step back?'.

Exceptions

Searching for times when the client was successful with the problem, if only to a small degree, is one of the most important therapeutic interventions. The therapist needs to become an expert in noticing differences between one point in time and another – for example, the beginning of therapy and the present time, or the beginning of the session and the current point in the session. Even minute differences should be highlighted because clients easily discount their efforts and spiral down into self-defeating patterns of thinking. Questions which externalise the problem and notice small wins can be coupled with consulting the client on their own progress. You might ask questions such as 'Which time stands out for you as the one where you really stood up to the influence of the bulimia?' and 'Are there times when you would expect the problem to happen, but it doesn't? How do you get that to happen?'. If the client cannot think of such a time, then I ask a circular question, inviting her consideration of exceptions from another's point of view – for example, 'If your brother were here, what would he say?' or 'What would your friend describe as a time when this problem could have got to you but you did something to prevent it? What would she or he say about how you did that?'.

Unique account questions

Each small win has to be amplified so that the client will break away from discounting and actually notice the way in which she has made progress. Unique account questions involve making exceptions meaningful. White (1991) calls this process 'historicising the unique account' and this means providing a new context for preferred stories about the client. These involve the client providing information about what happened, who was involved, where and when the event took place and her ideas as to why it took place. Examples here are 'How do you account for your ability to do this?'; 'Who would have been least surprised by this?'; 'What would your [friend, boyfriend] say if I was to ask them how they think you did this?'; 'Who would have been least surprised by this?'; 'What would your [friend, boyfriend] say if I was to ask him or her how she or he thinks you did this?'. Often these questions are reflexive, inviting an 'experience of experience'; that is, the client reflects on her own actions or thoughts or feelings, thereby highlighting the event, behaviour, thought or feeling as one worthy of consideration and encouraging self-awareness. You might ask, for example, 'What do you think of yourself having reduced the bingeing and vomiting?' or 'What do you think about yourself having spoken up to your boyfriend about your feelings?' This category of questions also asks about the opinion of a significant other: 'What would your mother have thought about you speaking up in this way?'.

Raising dilemmas

Sometimes clients feel very conflicted about solving a particular problem or moving forward in their lives. Raising dilemmas about whether to fight the problem can clarify its nature and assist the client to become clear about which direction she would like to go in. Raising dilemmas in the form of questions that posit two descriptions and that reflect the client's ambivalence about change should help here. The language selected is often biased towards one of the options and usually based on the therapist's hypothesis about the underlying developmental and interpersonal issues. The dilemma is often presented as two possible future developmental pathways; for example, 'Should you move forwards to a life where you are independent and trying out new and risky things, or should you mark time in a more dependent life, one where you need others' approval before you can try a new behaviour and where you must always look to others to get what you need?'.

Mapping effects of possible pathways

If the client poses a problem then I often encourage the exploration of the possible effects of client-proposed solutions over time – for example, 'What effect do you think choosing to do this would have on you or your relationship or the frequency of bingeing/purging?'. In addition I ask questions that encourage the client imaginatively to project herself forward in time in order to look back on her current decision – for example, 'If you were two years down the track, looking back on this decision, what do you think you would be advising yourself to do?'.

Restraining change

Client 'resistance' often happens because the client wants to protect her familiar identity and known world against perceived threat. If the problem begins to decrease in frequency and severity, sometimes clients can become alarmed because changes are happening too quickly for her to adjust. Once the client establishes a new direction by reducing the frequency of bingeing and vomiting or attempting change in another area of her life, I caution that she might be moving too fast and that perhaps she should slow down. This highlights the change process and the ascribing of control of the change process to the client, which is a very important aspect of addressing resistance as will be explained in Chapter Nine.

End of session message

At the close of each session, it is important to support your client in her openness to discuss her personal life and in her hope for improvement. Many have revealed a secret that they loathe and for which they feel ashamed. A simple acknowledgement can encourage clients to return and continue with a difficult process: for example, 'I appreciate your efforts in telling me about yourself' and 'Seeking help is hard but I feel it can also be a sign of strength'. The interview is concluded by a message. I often leave my office for five to ten minutes in order to construct it, explaining fully what I intend to do and why, and seeking permission from the client in doing so. When I return, the message usually takes the following format:

1. Compliments, to reinforce or acknowledge ways in which the client is taking charge of the problem. Here I often comment on character traits, intention of behaviour and/or steps already taken towards the solution: for example, 'You seem to be the kind of person who keeps going in spite of adversity – a real fighter. What makes me say this is…'.

2. Recount of exceptions to and successes over the problem; the purpose here is to help the client feel hopeful about the problem, to guide and empower her. Citing the ways in which the client has managed to decrease the level of bingeing and vomiting is important. Many clients have told me that focusing on their successes throughout the session, not only at the end, was the most important way of helping them through difficult times, particularly when they felt they had not had a good week – they had felt a failure before the session – and afterwards they were noticing ways in which they had improved.

3. Tasks or experiments – these were discussed in the previous chapter on effective tasks and interventions. However, one common first session task involves asking the client to pay attention to what happens to her (achievement of goals, family, life, marriage and so on) that she wants to continue to have happen. This builds a sense of inevitable change and allows people to notice that worthwhile things are presently happening. Here it might be useful to focus on clues, those behaviours that serve as hints to what the client may find helpful to continue to experiment with or to practise.

Therapeutic letters

I occasionally use letters that I write after the session has closed to reinforce ideas that have emerged during the session or to pose questions that I thought of after the client left. Letters are the brainchild of Michael White and David Epston (1989) and they mark a transition to narrative therapy in the development of systemic therapy generally. Clients are amazed that I have taken the trouble to do this and the letters can be instrumental in bringing an unsure client back to therapy. They can also be used to document progress over therapy marking the changes that have occurred, no matter how small.

Nylund and Thomas (1994) encourage a particular format in the therapist's letter to the client. There should be an introductory paragraph recounting highlights or what you found inspiring in the session, such as 'You were one of the few women with the problem I have ever known who wanted so badly to defeat the problem from the first moment she had it'. Then there should be a few statements or questions describing the influence of the problem on the client, and externalising it. 'Are you interested in moving forwards from this point, towards a life of self-determination, or is remaining captured by bulimia your preference, leading to a life that is forever imprisoned?'. Sometimes, Nylund and Thomas suggest that the best questions can occur to the therapist after the session: 'I wish I had asked you this question...'. It is a good idea to include such things in your letter – this will help to reinforce the client's interest and motivation to defeat the problem. Finally it is advised to document and highlight exceptions to the problem, using direct in-session quotes: 'When I asked if you had escaped the problem, do you remember you said "I am so strong"'.

This chapter has provided a general procedure for each session. Once again, the clients' individual needs are pre-eminent, so variations will occur. However, I have found the above framework to be robust across different situations, clients and conditions. It is now important to show the way in which these stages of treatment, tasks and interventions and general session procedure shown in the preceding three chapters can be implemented in the context of treatment. The following three case study chapters show the way in which the practices cited above are addressed in vivo. All identifying information has been changed to protect the privacy of the individuals concerned. The three women willingly gave their permission for me to include their stories in this book. For this, I appreciate their generosity and willingness to share themselves and their struggles for the benefit of others.

CHAPTER SIX

Case Study: Susanne

It became clear during the first session with Susanne, a 22-year-old photographic laboratory assistant, that she wished to talk about other problems in her life apart from the regular twice-weekly episodes of bingeing and purging. I attempted to explore the impact of the problem but she seemed reluctant to focus on the bulimia nervosa saying it was 'symptomatic of something deeper'. Her fear was that I would only concentrate on the bingeing and purging to the exclusion of all else. I showed her the test results she had completed in the period between the intake call and her first visit. Susanne's pre-test ratings on the Coopersmith Self-esteem Inventory placed her in the bottom 3 per cent of age-adjusted norms. She was moderately to mildly depressed according to her Beck Depression Scale scores and she showed elevated sub-scale scores on perfectionism, ineffectiveness and interoceptive awareness (which means the level of awareness in recognising and accurately identifying emotions or sensations of hunger and fullness) of the Eating Disorders Inventory (see Appendix for explanations of these texts). Susanne reviewed these findings and agreed that they accurately represented these areas of her functioning.

Susanne believed that all her problems were intricately tied to one another and that we could not work on one without working on the others. I assured her that I was willing to look at whatever issues she cared to present, that she would define the parameters of the discussion and we would work within those limits.

Consequently, most of the initial session swept over Susanne's range of problems from giving too much to men in her life to the disturbed, unhappy relationship with her parents and her low self-esteem, which she thought was linked in with the rejecting messages of her mother and the controlling influence of her father. She was in tears as she explained that she felt unworthy of ever being loved. Her mother once dispassionately told Susanne of her dismay at Susanne's conception and that she had tried to abort the pregnancy. Susanne had interpreted herself and her life in the light of this story of her rejection.

We spent some time in the initial session working out Susanne's goals. She definitely did not want to binge and purge any longer and when asked what she would be doing instead, she said she would feel much happier with her life. I asked her how she could bring this state about and she replied that she would be thinking about food when she was hungry, not obsessing about it most of the time as was the current situation. She was tearful as she described her next goal of facing her feelings. She often felt her feelings were 'inappropriate' for many situations, too strong and out of all proportion to the situation. She wanted to feel 'appropriately'. Her last goal was to do a lot more with her time; seeing friends, walking her dogs and horse riding.

At the beginning of the second session, Susanne was asked what it would be useful to talk about. At first, she did not know; I invited her to consider what her friend would advise talking about if she were there. Susanne promptly introduced the topic of the attitudes to, and valuing of, food in her family. We then looked at the influence of her family's attitudes on food on the development of her bulimic symptoms. She said that her mother had been on and off diets most of her life, and could look at any photo of herself and know exactly what she weighed. Her mother also practised some 'excessive food habits, being quite obsessive about food and weight'. We explored these and then I asked, 'How has your mother's dieting coached bad food habits in you?'. Susanne replied that she thought her mother's regimes with food made her more likely to diet which, in turn, made her more likely to binge. She also felt that her mother rewarded the children with food when this was not necessary. Susanne felt this was a way of controlling the children.

Susanne, referring now to herself, thought that she definitely had 'a thing about control. My last boyfriend said so many times "you're trying to control me" and I couldn't see that but I think there was something in it'. I asked her how important this controlling was in her life. She replied that if she did not do it, she 'would not be coping with my life at all'. She explained that it was not so much food that was bothering her any more but losing control of her feelings. She said feelings were on a much deeper level. Susanne told me she was close to losing control of her feelings a lot.

Susanne went on to speak of her father who was 'very self-controlled'. His attitude towards anything seemed to be 'if you want to do something, then just do it'. She said she thought he was scared of dying and tried to allay these fears by keeping fit. He seemed obsessive about petty things. He loathed the children standing in front of the fridge with the door open, worrying that the fridge would become icy. Susanne cried as she told me her father often rejected her.

The theme of rejection was taken up later in the session when, once again, Susanne said she was a 'shock' for her parents. When her mother found out she was pregnant with Susanne she 'did a few things to try to get rid of me.' I said, 'That must have been very painful for you to hear that,' and she sat silent and crying for a few moments. She said that her mother had always given conflicting messages: on the one hand 'I can cope with anything as supermum – I am highly achieving, high-powered and really together' as opposed to, on the other, 'I am not coping'. Another conflicting message was 'I don't want these three children' and 'I do want these three children'. This, coupled with the verbal message that her mother did not want her made Susanne's relationship with her parents very painful.

Susanne's 'overwhelming feelings' concerning certain situations surfaced again in our conversations. She described this as 'inappropriate amounts of feelings'. I asked her how she would know when her feelings were more appropriate to the situation. Susanne did not know so I persisted: 'What will be the first sign that you are reacting appropriately?' She said she would not experience such feelings of intense pain and loneliness. Susanne said that she was 'working in her own darkroom' as far as her feelings were concerned. Later, I asked her what would happen if she turned on the light in the darkroom and she replied that she had already but there were still some 'dark corners'. I acknowledged her courage in facing such pain and asked whether she had insights when she turned on the light. Susanne said that her mother considered it a real strength of character not to talk about feelings. I asked how had she managed to stand up to her mother's rejection by speaking up about her feelings. She sat still for a while.

In my message at the end of this session, I externalised the problem by saying that I was impressed with the way she had reacted so promptly when she saw the bulimia nervosa was trying to get control of her life. I said the bulimia nervosa seemed to be an indirect way of reminding her about the 'rejection' and the 'inappropriateness' of feelings so that she could resolve them. Susanne added that her mother rewarded her 'inappropriately' – that she often mixed up food and love and that she had an 'inappropriate' focus on food, weight and self-control. In order to separate from the themes of rejection and inappropriateness we had to separate other things in her life. We also needed to gain some knowledge and control of the bingeing and vomiting; I asked her to do the following:

1. to notice which days she was being appropriate about feelings and which days she was not. She was asked to write these down

2. to notice when she was hungry and when she was not

3. to spend at least ten minutes a day doing something she used to enjoy. If she could not think of anything, she was to do something different from what she always did. I characterised her depression as attempting to reject herself – another way of

reminding her of a story from her past – and so doing something enjoyable each day was caring for and affirming herself

4. to think about food if she felt like having a binge and to observe the reasons why she binged. This would provide us with more information

5. to keep an account of the binge. I suggested she record the quantity and type of food, events occurring before and after and the people involved.

As control seemed an important issue for Susanne, I gave a number of suggested tasks as opposed to a single task in order to encourage her sense of choice in the counselling process.

Much of the third session was spent discussing responses to the tasks set in the previous session. Susanne had been ill with the flu for most of the week and she coughed throughout the session, which was cut short as a consequence. Susanne began by saying she had been very ill during the week and that she had not binged or vomited. I highlighted this exception to the pattern of bingeing and purging by asking her how she managed not to binge or vomit. Susanne said that she had felt close to vomiting on Monday but that she disliked the physical sensation of vomiting so much that she was not prepared to begin. Encouraging her perception of a sense of control over the bulimic symptoms, I asked 'Does this new event suggest you are more in control or less in control of the bingeing?'. Susanne replied, 'More in control, although I was too sick to really binge'.

We also reviewed Susanne's response to the task of spending ten minutes a day doing something enjoyable. I asked her to scale her feelings before and after the task along a continuum where one represented not feeling good and ten represented feeling superb. She had been horse riding, canoeing and walking her dogs. Although she only answered the scaling question for horse riding she said she had really enjoyed it despite her negative feelings before going out. I invited her to predict what would happen if she continued with these activities, and whether she would find them more or less enjoyable. Susanne smiled cautiously and answered, 'More enjoyable'.

Susanne then began to speak of her 'restlessness' and 'unhappiness' about herself. She said she often felt lonely when she went to another person's house and they were not there (as in visiting her parents and finding no one home). She said she did not know why and I asked a circular question, 'Who of all the people you know might be able to tell you why?'. She finally said that her girlfriend Chris might know why: Chris might say she was 'missing out'. When I asked missing out on what, she replied that she often reached out to console others rather than herself. I acknowledged that giving to herself was one way of not 'missing out'. I asked her what effect reaching out to console others had on her restlessness and unhappiness. Susanne thought that she really wanted to reach out to others to console herself. I asked her whether, if she reached out to others about her own problems rather than theirs, she would still be missing out. How much light would this let into her 'dark room'? She replied that it would be wonderful. I then asked whether, if she told Chris, her girlfriend, about her problems, this would be part of reaching out to others so that they could be there for her? Susanne thought it 'would certainly make them closer'.

In my message at the end of the session, I said that I was impressed by the way that Susanne was beginning to let 'more light inside' and I was looking forward to seeing some of the effects that this would have on her life in the near future.

I then asked her to:

1. continue with ten minutes a day doing something she used to enjoy – only this time, something different from the week before

2. notice which days of the week were 'appropriate' and which days were not in relation to her sense of having the appropriate amount of feelings for a given situation

3. think about the binge beforehand if she felt she was going to have one

4. notice when she was hungry and when she was not and try an experiment – that is, to eat when she was hungry. At the end, Susanne said that having to articulate the signs of her own hunger in response to my question 'How will you know when you are hungry?' led her to conclude that she was filling her 'vague emptiness with food'.

At the next session, Susanne had not binged or vomited since our last session two weeks before. In response to the previous session's tasks, she found she experienced 'inappropriate' feelings on only one day and when she thought about those feelings, she realised that they were quite appropriate. Susanne said that thinking about her feelings made them lose their power over her; not thinking about them gave them energy. I watched Susanne as she spoke of her response to the tasks and noticed that she was far less tearful than in our previous sessions. She spoke with greater assurance, her voice stronger and more evenly modulated. Her sentences were carried firmly through to a confident end. I wondered aloud if the problem was the inappropriateness or her 'beating herself up' about the inappropriateness. I commented that she was making up for lost time in nurturing herself.

Susanne said she would like to talk more about her 'inappropriate' feelings, so I asked her how she judged whether her feelings were appropriate or inappropriate. Although we both felt encouraged by her recent triumph over 'beating herself up' about inappropriateness, Susanne quickly returned to speaking about an incident when her boyfriend said he would be home by a certain time and he actually came home some hours later. She felt she over-reacted to the situation and said she should not have worried about it. I clarified this by asking, 'When John says he is going to do something and he does not do this, do you think your anger and hurt is inappropriate?' She replied that she should be quite happy to wait for him. I asked, 'How will you know when he is going to be coming or not?' Susanne then said she felt a certain ambivalence – she was not sure if she should expect John to keep his promises or if she should 'wield a big stick'. I agreed that this was a central issue and I wondered out loud how coming to terms with it would affect Susanne's evaluation of the appropriateness of her feelings. I suggested she return to the issue of judging whether her feelings were appropriate or not.

I asked her what would happen if she spoke about her feelings. Susanne felt that she had a right to ask him to keep his promises but that this made it likely that she would express her displeasure and perhaps be perceived by John as a 'demanding lover'. We tried to work out what it was about being a demanding lover that would really bother her and how she could tell her feelings without damaging the relationship. I asked her whether she felt that she should not demand or expect anything from him and whether this was part of her rule of being there for others, while others did not have to be there for her. She said it probably was.

When we returned to the original issue of judging inappropriate and appropriate feelings, I asked whether she thought her feelings on this occasion were more or less appropriate in light of what we had discussed. Susanne replied, 'I guess they were appropriate – more so'. It was just how they were expressed.

Collapsing time, I asked 'What effect do you think focusing on your own needs will have on your relationship with John, say, over the next six months?' Susanne thought that it would have a positive effect, in fact, a 'gradual improvement' in their relationship in that she would be focused on herself and less demanding of John. His responses, although important to her, would be far less 'earth-shattering'. She also thought that focusing on her own needs would make her far less likely to be jealous about John's other relationships.

Susanne then turned the conversation to her bingeing. She told me how she had thoughts of having a binge after eating. We worked out that it was her distended stomach that provoked thoughts of a binge. She felt self-loathing after feeling the abdominal bulge. We renamed this bulge the 'rounded stomach' and talked for some time how the 'rounded stomach' was normal after a meal. Susanne said she had talked herself out of bingeing. I asked her how she had managed to defy the perception of the 'rounded stomach' and what it asked her to do. Susanne said she became really defiant and had simply refused to give in to it.

I then asked, 'Who would have been least surprised by this defiance?' At first, she did not know, then she said her past boyfriend Alan, who had often said she was fine and that the 'rounded stomach' did not matter to him. I asked, 'What did he know about you then that would have led him to predict this defiance?' Susanne replied that he would have noticed that she was courageous and that she spoke out about her needs.

Turning to another of the tasks, Susanne reported that on the majority of days, she did something enjoyable each day and focused on herself and affirmed herself. I asked about the effects of this on her self-esteem. Susanne said it had a big effect, raising her awareness of her feelings, and that she realised more that her feelings were quite appropriate. Susanne felt that poetry was particularly useful for helping her work out her feelings. We talked about her poetry and how it helped her to see what she was really feeling. I invited Susanne to consider the effects of doing these kinds of activities over time: 'If you continued to work out your feelings over the next few weeks, do you think you would be more likely to feel better or less likely?' She replied that she would be more likely. Susanne thought that thinking about her feelings would make them lose their power – not thinking about them gave them energy. She reiterated her original intention in that she wanted to be fully conscious of 'underlying issues'.

In my message at the end of the session, I said I was impressed by her speaking up for her feelings with John. I wondered, if she continued to speak up for her feelings, what effect that would have on her 'eating over them' with the binges. I asked Susanne to:

1. notice when she was thinking about food and when she was not and to notice whether thinking about food was connected to the 'grumbling stomach', that is, actual feelings of hunger

2. continue with ten minutes a day doing something she used to enjoy – only this time 'doing something different' from the

previous week in order to notice what effect this had on satisfying her needs

3. become obsessed about food if she was intent on bingeing and keep an account of the binge.

At the beginning of session five, Susanne sat forward in her chair, asking about my physical and emotional well-being. Then she told me she had not binged and vomited; that she had not even felt a 'vague urge'. The task of recognising when she was hungry and when she was not was particularly useful. She saw now that she had often confused hunger with emotional upset, that she would have thoughts about food when she was hungry and that these thoughts about food were a signal to eat. She said this 'normalised her eating patterns'. I was curious about how she knew she was hungry. We both laughed when she said 'I have a gurgling, grumbling stomach'.

She said she was having trouble focusing on herself whenever her boyfriend was around. She said that she had a tendency to 'lose herself' whenever John was around. I reframed her concern as a sign that she was willing to allow him to come closer to her, and that this may have brought opportunities for her to sort out her boundaries with him. Susanne then said that she was looking more and more towards herself in order to be happy rather than depending on him. Abruptly changing the conversation, Susanne said she really wanted to discuss something.

She began by saying she often experienced sudden mood changes. She clarified this by saying that these moods took the form of 'low energy, feeling depressed and miserable and sometimes over-whelming feelings, either the wrong feeling for the situation or too much of the feeling'. There did not appear to be any triggering events and she felt she did not have any 'tangible reason for being miserable'. At this point in the session, Susanne became very tearful. She said she experienced very disturbing images. I asked what she saw and she replied that she saw a big dark scary figure with an erection and that she felt very small. She thought that it might be her father.

Susanne once again said she was concerned that she was inventing these images in an attempt to find a tangible reason for her misery. She seemed ambivalent about pursuing these images. I said I did not know what these images meant for her; they could have many meanings – for example, pre-verbal memories of actual sexual abuse or visual symbols of unnamed fears. I asked if she wanted to let these images in and know what they were about or if she would prefer to go on not knowing what they were. She said she was willing to find out but she was scared: 'The images have been on top of me for quite a few years – it's time to face a lot of things.'

I asked Susanne how she would handle it if she did let the images in and discovered sexual abuse. She replied that she was 'fairly rational'. The worst thing was not knowing – it was a fear of her fear that bothered her. I attempted to encapsulate her fear and suggest a way out by asking whether she had ever lain in bed at night as a child and thought there were vague amorphous monsters under the bed. She said that she had and that she worried if she left a hand dangling they would pull her down under with them. I then asked if she had ever got up and turned on the light and looked under the bed to see what was there. She said that she had done this on several occasions. So I asked her, if she turned on the light with the misery and looked under the bed, what effect this would have on the misery. Susanne said that it would be no worse than not looking, and that 'it would help to not let the misery control my life. An unnamed fear has more power because it is unnamed.' She spontaneously added that 'it is time to consciously invite these images in – they keep knocking at the door anyway'. She went on to describe an incident from her mid-adolescence when she nearly killed herself with alcohol and was admitted to intensive care. She said her mother would not even talk to her. The family doctor recommended that she see a psychologist who subsequently pronounced the family 'normal'.

I tentatively asked Susanne whether she wanted to explore these unnamed fears now or at some time in the future, and she deter-minedly said that she would explore them now. She closed her eyes and said she had an image of someone like her father putting his finger in and out of her vagina. She said she was frightened and hurt and crying and that she felt like a baby. I asked, if the baby could talk what would she say? Susanne said she would want to be loved, that she would want to be filled up with love – 'that was what the bulimia nervosa was about – a baby feeling so empty'.

I asked Susanne how she could care for the baby. She replied, 'by being calm and quiet and not rushing around'. I asked her to wrap her adult body around the curled tense frightened body of the baby, to cradle the baby in a calm and quiet way. She did so for some time, sitting and smiling, and with her face and body visibly relaxed. I asked what had become of the frightening image, and she replied that it had gone and her eyes gradually opened. She said that she felt better and that she was getting a lot out of our sessions. I asked, 'What effect will being in touch with Small Susanne's needs have on Big Susanne's misery?' She replied that it would probably have an effect but she was not sure. She said she felt 'really good.' We sat in silence until I said that if the frightening images returned, I hoped she would feel comfortable to talk about them. We still did not know what they meant but Susanne was open to finding out as time went on. I did not give a task in this session as Susanne was winning in her fight with bulimia nervosa. I thought it more appropriate to highlight her wins and encourage her to do more of the same.

In the sixth session, Susanne said she had not binged or vomited since our last session. When I asked what it would be useful to talk about, Susanne replied that she had been feeling 'really happy and loved and loving'. She also said she hadn't been feeling depressed. I asked her if that was different from before, and she replied, 'definitely'. She said she was 'dealing more directly with the underlying issues that might be causing the bulimia in the first place'. This more direct dealing with her feelings was occurring more frequently, and she did not feel that she was ignored or misunderstood – she did not feel like a 'yawning cavern' any more.

She said that she was eating 'very normally, more normally than I have for years but I still worry about putting on weight. I haven't at all thought – if I binge I'll feel better as a way of dealing with it. 'Cause that's in the past.' Susanne added, 'I'm certainly moving in the right direction.'

I asked her how she accounted for the change and Susanne said, 'the last few sessions have influenced my moods. It is hard to put it into words – I have just felt happier inside. John and I are getting on well. I'm aware more quickly when I'm blocking emotional things, although I have to really concentrate to let my emotions in because my mind keeps wandering off.'

I asked whether she was more or less comfortable than before our sessions about letting her emotions in, and she replied that she was more comfortable and less frightened. She also said that when she felt disturbed she needed 'to be alone to think about the feeling'. I asked what she had done in the past to get in touch with disturbed feelings and she replied that she probably would have gone out and found someone to nurture. I asked whether she was tending to nurture herself more and Susanne replied that she was 'beginning' to.

She said she had to work on her self-esteem in order to keep nurturing herself, and that her low self-esteem was 'behind every-thing'. I asked her if nurturing other people was a way of ignoring herself and she replied that it was a distraction, like watching TV – that is, getting involved in the 'soap operas of other people's lives'. Had she ever allowed others to be there for her? She said it always came as a surprise when others were there for her. In a small voice, she said she did not have many friends any more, although her relation-ship with John was going better – she was not nurturing him as much. She said a number of times during the interview that she had not been enjoying work very much.

She said she knew that she deserved respect but that this was only a superficial belief. Deep down she said she did not really believe it. I suggested that these thoughts must be very painful to her and asked how long she had been duped by rejection. She replied, 'nearly all my life.' She described the process as letting things get to a certain point because she did not feel good inside, but they would not get beyond that point because 'my logic can't ignore it'. She would not let people walk all over her. I asked, 'Is your logic more like an ally in your fight against rejection in that it won't let you get beyond a certain point?' She replied, 'Yes ... I keep doing all the nurturing and then I reach a point when I want something back.'

Susanne then told me that about seven years ago she had decided to abandon her logic because she lived too much 'in her head'. She was more logical then so she decided to let her emotional side in more. I said I was curious that she saw these two centres in either-or terms and wondered about the notion of a 'thinking heart', one that named an emotion and evaluated how to come to terms with it. Susanne speculated that not naming her emotional life nor trying to satisfy it was 'the major thing keeping me back' and said that she felt it would have profound effects on her self-esteem and her relationships. She also said she would often put John's needs first and that undermined the relationship in that she would gradually become resentful.

In my message at the end of the session, I suggested that in abandoning her thinking centre, she had robbed herself of a fertile base from which to operate in the world. I said that it seemed to me that operating from both the logic centre and the emotional or feeling centre allows a fuller experience and expression of life. I told her that allowing logic back into her life might protect her from feelings that, when allowed to grow wild, destroy all the beauty in the garden – it seemed that the cultivation of a 'thinking heart' might protect her from 'too wild' feelings.

I added that this was only my opinion and that it might be good to make some experiments in the next few days. These experiments would contrast living a life 'without logic' and living a life 'with logic'. I suggested that, if one day she was feeling disturbed, she should not name the feelings nor try to work out why she was feeling that way. I asked her to see what effect this had on her relationship with John (if the upset feeling was concerned with John). On another day, she was to name the feeling she was experiencing, find some way of satisfying it and notice what effect this had on her relationship with John. In addition, in response to several comments she had made during the session about her lack of friends, we decided that Susanne would recontact her friends at least twice during the week.

At the beginning of session seven, Susanne said she had not binged or vomited in the three weeks since I had seen her. However, she said she had been very upset and depressed for two and a half of those three weeks. She had lots of hassles with her boyfriend, John, and she had been feeling very unhappy in her job. She told me she resigned from her job the previous day. She said that she was in a senior position in the photographic firm and the next step for her career would be a management position that she felt she probably could get, but would not really want. She found her work un-challenging and unrewarding. Her feelings were complicated by the fact that her boyfriend was working in a similar position at the same firm.

Susanne also said that John did not satisfy her needs, he did not know how to be nurturing and that he did not 'give' in the same way that she did. She added that she felt a great deal of instability in her life in a rented cottage in the countryside. At sheep-shearing time each year and at a moment's notice, she must vacate her house for occupation by the shearers for a period of up to three weeks. To top it off, her dog had died the previous week. I reframed her depression as coming to a crossroads where many decisions were being made: whether to leave the job; whether to end the relationship with John; what new career direction to pursue; and what to do about the insta-bility of her domestic situation. It seemed too that she had to leave behind her old life with her dog.

I asked Susanne which of the issues she would find useful to talk about and she replied, her career. However, when we began to talk, John soon reappeared as the topic for discussion. I called attention to this and she decided they were, after all, interconnected. She told me she was tired of her 'wild and emotional reactions to insignificant incidents'. I asked her to describe a typical and recent situation where she felt this to be the case. She recounted an incident where John had made a remark about a woman who is the 'lady of the house' where he boards. He told this woman that she had 'a lovely body' and Susanne had felt jealous and had 'played a few games'. She went on to describe one of the games. A short time after her conversation with John, he asked her to go back to his house and she said no. He left. She went after him, found him and they spent the night together.

I commented, 'those jealous voices must be so painful to you'. Susanne was silent, then looked at me, saying she was surprised by my comment and that 'thinking about them in this way is different for me'. I said that thinking about them in this way might help to widen the gap between the event and her reaction and, hopefully, introduce an element of choice. She agreed and I asked what she thought she needed to widen the gap. Susanne said 'control', and I added 'imagination, too' – the imagination to fantasise different ways of responding that were not doomed to repeat her past.

I asked if her depression was coupled with a period of 'wild emotional reactions' and she replied, 'Yes'. I wondered aloud about her needs going unmet in a relationship and that this is coupled with her painful thoughts about not deserving love. These painful thoughts restrain her from speaking up for her needs that seem to build up until they come out as wild. Susanne called them 'feral feelings' and we both laughed. I wondered if a secondary problem had grown up around the original problem in that Susanne then felt depressed about her outbursts.

In my message at the end of the session, I said I was concerned that she might be moving too fast by trying to confront all the big issues in her life at once – relationship, career, house. I suggested that maybe she should slow down in her improvement, take it easy and not push herself with so many decisions – perhaps she should dawdle at the crossroads for a while. Susanne quickly said she was 'comfortable with our pacing'.

I also suggested the possibility of a relapse, saying it was likely that life events would sometimes conspire to make her vulnerable to her voices – 'voices that say you are not good enough for other people, that your needs are not as important'. I also said that relapses were normal when moving in a new direction. I asked what resources she had to deal with relapses. We spent some time naming them. She said that determining the kind of hunger she was feeling and then doing something about it really helped her. She also mentioned speaking up about her needs.

The tasks for the next sessions were to name the feeling she was having and to see whether John was the appropriate person to be satisfying the feeling or should it be something or someone else. I also asked her to think about what she could call a purpose in her current life – something she wanted to do. I asked her to write down her fantasies about what she would like to do, to be and to have in her life and then to circle three of these that seemed possible and challenging.

Our final session was four weeks later. Susanne's depression had abated and she said that this was '…very different from before'. She said that occasionally she felt 'depressed, but mostly I feel very even-keeled'. She added that she felt 'a great deal more choice' and that this was different from before the commencement of therapy. Susanne also said she knew when she was 'being appropriate in her feelings and actions now' because she felt she had more options. She told me that she had binged/vomited twice in the past four to five weeks. She said this was mostly due to the pressures of work and the decision to leave work. She disliked being at work but felt an allegiance to her boss who had been kind to her in the past. She felt she needed to stay for another month even although this was making her feel stressed. During the session Susanne repeated these thoughts many times.

She had made an unsuccessful late attempt to apply for entry to a university. She would apply the following semester. She said she also needed to start thinking about applying for a new job. Her current job pressures were demanding but she felt fine generally and that was really different from before. When I asked what the difference was, Susanne said she felt that there were more options in between something happening and her reaction. She felt 'a great deal more choice' and this was different from before the commencement of therapy. Susanne also said she knew when she was 'being appropriate in my feelings and actions now' because she felt she had more options. She felt she had more of a choice about acting on hurt feelings; she was less their victim. She spoke up for her feelings with friends and associates, telling them how she felt; John and many others had responded to these changes by being 'more available' to Susanne and 'more helpful'.

The problem of appropriate feelings for different situations was no longer an issue. She also said she was far more prepared to 'risk being wrong' with decisions in her relationships and life choices. She said that her goals were a lot clearer and that making new career decisions had made an 'enormous difference' to her feelings about herself. I highlighted these differences and normalised the relapse by saying that people sometimes find they relapse when they embark on a new direction. In fact, it was a highly probable event seeing they had spent so much time in the past dealing with stress in this way. We again discussed her resources for dealing with the problem if it were to recur.

Given the short-term benefits of bulimia nervosa in dealing with stress, it was no wonder that she had relapsed in such a difficult period. However we both knew bulimia nervosa had dangerous long-term consequences that worked their way into a vicious cycle. I suggested that the binge-eating and vomiting was a way to reduce tension. It served to dull Susanne's senses so that she did not feel as keenly and it also distracted her from her feelings.

In my message at the end of the session, I said that the fact that bingeing and vomiting were effective in the short term posed a dilemma. Should Susanne pursue dealing with her feelings indirectly because it is effective in the short term or should she deal more directly with her feelings because it was better in the long term? Susanne immediately replied that she wanted 'a more direct life'.

I then asked her to try an experiment. She agreed and so I asked her the next time she felt vague, restless, unhappy and tense to do something different. She spontaneously replied that she would yell or put on a loud record and dance. Susanne then said she felt 'much better' and did not think she would need to come to see me any more. We discussed our time together and marked out all the different ways in which she had managed to get on top of the problem. I asked how she would remind herself of all the resources available to her if she came upon another difficult passage in her life. Her answer surprised me: 'I will read through all my writing and poetry'. She then spent some time talking about the tasks she had tried between sessions, saying that they were a very important aspect of getting on top of the bingeing and vomiting, that they gave her a sense of movement along the path to health and 'something to be working on' in the slower middle parts of therapy. The timing of these tasks was very important. They dealt with the confusion as it occurred, 'addressing a problem as it arose'. Tasks that dealt with her obsession with food showed her that she was not obsessed with food; thoughts of food were 'just normal signs of hunger'. In relation to her 'feral' feelings, she realised that it was not wrong to feel emotional, that her reactions were often quite appropriate. Susanne said the tasks were also useful in that they broke large issues down into 'dealable pieces'. Her next comment was revealing; she confessed that she did the tasks to please me, especially initially, and that she may not have done them if I had not firmly suggested them, particularly the 'enjoyable ones'. I said at least there were some benefits from her old habit of being there for others. I thanked her for letting me be close to her. I finished by saying she could come back if she ever needed me.

At post-counselling, Susanne's self-esteem rating on the Coopersmith Self-esteem Inventory had risen to the upper 15 per cent which is indicative of very high self-esteem. The rating was maintained at long-term follow-up assessment, three months later.

Her score on the Beck Depression Inventory similarly showed a dramatic improvement, scoring well within normality. This improvement was also maintained at long-term follow-up. There was an improvement at post-counselling for all sub-scale scores on the Eating Disorder Inventory except perfectionism. Fortunately, this sub-scale improved at long-term follow-up.

CHAPTER SEVEN

Case Study: Marie

Beverly, Marie's mother, initially contacted me by telephone asking for help because her daughter had recently revealed she was bulimic. Beverly sounded anxious as she told me the circumstances of her daughter's disclosure. Inviting a close elderly friend around for lunch, Beverly discussed the health risks of bulimia nervosa and anorexia nervosa while Marie was occupied but within listening distance. After the conversation, Marie came to her mother confessing that she was bingeing and vomiting daily. Marie cried when she told her mother that no matter how hard she tried, she could not stop the behaviour and that she was disgusted with herself.

Beverly then told me that she had been sick for two years with Myoencephalitis Syndrome (although she still worked) and that she felt partly responsible for Marie's problem as she was often not available for the children. Marie lived with Ben, her father, Beverly her mother, and Lawrie, her 14-year-old brother. Ben, Beverly's husband, was rarely at home, his job necessitating regular interstate travel. A stilted hesitancy in the way she relayed this information suggested there were difficulties in the marital relationship. She went on to say that he often returned home at weekends to be with the family. I attempted to reassure Beverly by explaining that many different and interacting factors seem to predispose people to the problem of bulimia nervosa and that attributing 'blame' to any member of the family was not part of the therapeutic process we would use, nor was it useful or necessary for Marie's progress.

I invited her and the other family members to come to some of the sessions if Marie desired this, suggesting that their attendance would be helpful in 'supporting Marie in throwing off the bulimia nervosa'. She said that, as yet, the other members of the family did not know about Marie's problem but she was going to tell Ben soon. Beverly was happy to come to the initial session; Marie had already asked her to do so.

Marie was 17 years old when I first met her, and bingeing and vomiting an average of 14 times a week. Dark, short and good-looking, she presented in baggy clothes that disguised what seemed to be a slightly larger than average shape. She seemed shy, rarely making eye contact with me and looking lost in the strange surroundings of my office. During the entire first session, Marie and Beverly sat huddled close together on the sofa in my office. Beverly initially dominated the conversation although, after about half an hour, she periodically looked blank and stared out of the window, allowing space for her daughter's comments. They confirmed what Beverly had told me on the phone about Marie's disclosure of her bulimic behaviour.

The bulimic behaviour had begun four years previously when Marie was 13. Marie said it started as a way to control her weight and that she first heard about bingeing and vomiting through friends at school. The behaviour occurred sporadically at first but then increased quickly to the current frequency. Marie said that she must keep slim because others would not like her if she was overweight. When I asked who would not like her, she said her friends would laugh at her and boys would not ask her out. Like many girls her age, she felt she must conform to current fashion dictates for pencil-thin slimness in order to be acceptable to others.

Marie's pre-counselling ratings on the Coopersmith Self-esteem Inventory placed her in the bottom 5 per cent on age-adjusted norms for women of her age. She was moderately depressed according to her pre-counselling scores on the Beck Depression Scale. Her scores on the Eating Disorder Inventory were elevated on the sub-scales drive

for thinness, bulimia, body dissatisfaction, ineffectiveness and interoceptive awareness compared to the norms for anorexic and bulimic
women (see Appendix for explanations of these tests). Marie confirmed these results, saying she had never felt so low.

I asked Marie to outline her goals for her therapy: 'How will you
know that you are over the bulimia? What will you notice you are
doing differently?' Marie negatively defined her goals as being free
from bingeing and vomiting. When asked to state these in more
positive terms – 'What will you be doing instead?' – she said she
would go out a lot more, study a bit more and learn to play tennis.

Each goal was rated on a scale from one to ten. Marie nominated a
number where she felt she was currently, another number where she
would like to be and what she wanted to do in the next week to take
her just one or two steps closer to where she wanted to be. For
example, with studying a little more, Marie felt she was at a three,
with one representing not enough studying and ten representing an
excellent amount of studying. She wanted to be a nine and was
prepared to make a start towards this by taking a step towards a five. I
asked what she would be doing differently at a five and she said
sitting down regularly each night to study for a specified period.

Given Marie's shyness, it was important to establish rapport early
on in the sessions. Eliciting Marie's goals in the initial session helped
to align with where she wanted to go in her life and it also encouraged
her to be active in the therapeutic process. Her participation in the
session seemed to grow when she, not I, defined the parameters of the
discussion. Marie's goals assisted her to invest in her own future.

During this initial session, I externalised the problem as 'the
bulimia' many times, encouraging Marie to separate from the problem
and to review her relationship with it. I asked her what kinds of habit
bulimia nervosa had coached in her. She replied that the problem
meant that she was having showers three times a day (she would
vomit in the shower). It also meant that she was brushing her teeth
three times a day. She then said the bulimia stopped her from eating
certain foods – she could not eat cheese, milk, lollies, toast, and

yoghurt because these were 'horrible foods' to vomit up. Marie said she often ate frozen food and raw pasta. Beverly commented on the times when she found half-empty packets of frozen peas and beans in the freezer or went to the food cupboard and found recently bought but one-quarter empty packets of pasta. They both laughed at this, although Marie's mother's laughter seemed in good humour while Marie looked away, more than a little embarrassed at the description.

I then asked Marie to map her influence in the life of the problem: 'What effect have you had in trying to beat the bulimia?' Marie went on to describe a number of delay and substitution strategies that were effective for her. Calling her mother at work if she was feeling tempted to binge and vomit proved to be an ally in the fight against bulimia. Although she did not explain the reason for the call to Beverly, she found it comforting to talk to her mother at these times. Marie also said that she found going to the beach for a few days helpful because she enjoyed it so much, the sun and surf occupying her mind. Going to the city, playing tennis in the afternoon, lying on her bed and listening to music and watching a good video were other ways she managed to have some influence over the problem. She found she could 'put the bingeing and vomiting off for a while' if she did these things.

Highlighting these exceptions, I asked Beverly, 'Is this a surprise to you that Marie has some influence over the bulimia?' Beverly said she was 'not surprised at all' and that Marie was really a 'most determined person'. She felt that Marie could do whatever was needed to get on top of the problem. Beverly, until this moment quietly observing, then became quite animated, declaring that the bulimia nervosa had some influence over her. I asked what habits the problem had coached in Beverly. She said she had developed the habit of asking too many questions about it when Marie got home. I said it was quite common for a family member to participate inadvertently in the continuation of the problem and no fault of their own. Marie's mother was partici-pating in Marie's problem by questioning Marie every time she went to the toilet or had a shower, because she was afraid Marie had vomited. I asked Marie what effect this questioning had on her. She replied that it made her guilty and feel like doing it more. Although well-meaning, the questioning promoted an escalation of the behaviour.

I was curious about the beginnings of this questioning trend. Beverly said she did not know exactly when it began but that it was probably fairly close to the time when Marie told her about the bulimia. Locating this trend over time, I asked Beverly whether she thought the questioning was happening more or less often these days. Marie answered quickly, 'more often'. I asked Marie if she felt the questioning made the bulimia more likely to continue or to lessen. Marie replied: 'More likely to continue.'

We then talked about Beverly's concern for Marie and I reframed and externalised Beverly's concern as a 'vulnerability to guilt' about Marie's problem. While wanting to show that Beverly was inadvertently participating in the problem, I did not want her to feel guilty. I believe that therapists need to be wary here, given women's attribution of blame to themselves for problems in the family. Any questions implicitly invoking blame become a breeding ground for self- recrimination. I asked Beverly, 'How does your vulnerability to guilt invite you to be responsible for Marie's problem?' Beverly said she was worried about Marie and wanted her to be better and not to have the bulimia.

I wondered out loud if this interaction concerning the problem could be a way of showing Marie and her mother their ambivalence in moving from one life stage to another. Beverly had to separate from Marie and allow her to take charge of her own life and Marie had to resist the temptation to rely on mother's answers to her problems. In this way, the symptoms seemed to function as a way of keeping Marie from taking the risks necessary for the successful passage from dependence to independence. I asked Marie and Beverly, 'Should Marie step back from the problem and let Beverly own it, or should Beverly step back from the problem and let Marie own it?' Both agreed that it was better if Marie owned the problem. I then asked

'What effect would Marie owning the problem have on Marie?' Both thought that it would help Marie grow up.

Searching for exceptions to Beverly's uninvited involvement, I asked her if there were times when she had managed to escape the guilt and not get involved. She replied that sometimes she felt like saying something to Marie but refrained. I asked her how she managed this and she replied that it was very hard but she had gone and done something else instead.

Towards the end of the session I asked them what had been the most beneficial aspects of it. Beverly said that she had not realised how much the bulimia had influenced her to 'take command of Marie's life by questioning too much' and that she had not fully realised the effect the questioning was having on the problem. Marie said she felt more determined than ever to defeat the bulimia and that she realised what a 'disgusting habit' it was. I asked Marie how she felt about coming again; she was undecided and needed time to think. I said I was available and that she could call when ready.

Beverly rang back a few days later saying that Marie would like to come and see me regularly but she was afraid that I 'would not like her'. I sent a short letter to Marie recapping our first session together and then saying that her comment surprised me because I was not sure if she liked me! It was an honest response and I sensed it would contribute to a sense of fit, of connection between us which was contrary to the original tenor of our relationship. Initially, Marie seemed to invite a firm complementary relationship with me. She was anxious to be 'cured' and wanted me to undertake the roles of leader and expert. In the next session, I wanted to encourage more symmetrical possibilities between us. I hoped that this movement between symmetricality and complementarity would encourage her flexibility and allow me to shift between roles with her. It was important for Marie to start assuming responsibility for her life – otherwise I would take over mother's role in assuming responsibility for her future.

The following week Marie came to the session alone as previously arranged. She reported in a defeated manner that she had binged and vomited four times since the last session. I asked her how she had managed to drastically reduce the bingeing and vomiting. Marie said she was surprised by this question. She thought she was going 'really badly' but the question made her think that I did not think she was going too badly at all. I reframed Marie's defeat as a victory, highlighting her 'win' over the problem.

Marie answered my original question by saying 'not looking in the food cupboards and doing lots of homework'. She said that she had stayed at school during the free period and sat with friends. This had been a difficult time for the battle with the bulimia as, prior to the beginning of therapy, she would go home and binge and vomit. Marie also said that she reminded herself not to do it and that this had worked for her. She said she made herself go out more, sleep a lot and lie down and rest if she felt like bingeing. She said she often thought about something else (mostly boys) when she lay in bed.

I then introduced the idea that the bulimia 'fed on secrecy', suggesting that the problem seemed to grow bigger the more it was kept a secret and it seemed to grow smaller when it was shared with others. Marie readily identified with this idea and said she would like to tell the rest of the family, even though she was scared.

Marie talked for the majority of the session about a boy she liked. She liked thinking about him and she felt this really helped in 'winning over the bulimia'. Talking about her interest in boys helped to further the rapport between us. Marie's interest in boys was actually a large part of her experience. I felt that I needed to listen, even though this was not part of her initial problem nor a stated explicit goal. Ultimately, Marie's interest in boys presented itself as an indirect pathway to beating bulimia nervosa. Marie would often lie on her bed thinking about boys, rather than bingeing and purging!

It became obvious during this session that I needed to shift fluidly from 'expert' to 'confidant'. I believe it was this fluidity that allowed Marie to treat me as a friend who would share her secrets and allow her room to explore her needs. It eventually led to an exploration of her concern for her personality, appearance and desirability, which were key issues in the development of her bulimic behaviour.

In this session, Marie revealed to me that she was very shy, often feeling scared with people, especially boys, and worrying about whether they liked her. She did not feel that she had much going for her – not good looks nor a vibrant personality. She dressed in baggy clothes because she was afraid her friends would mock her if she were not slim and beautiful. She said she was 'too scared' to show them her shape. I externalised the problem by asking, 'How has the shyness got in the way of you living the life that you would like to live?'. Marie said the shyness kept her from going out and kept her from getting along with friends.

We talked about the history and culture of the current dictates of slimness and fashion and the effect it was having on young women's lives. Marie had traded her determination and individuality for perceived acceptance by her peers. Her self-consciousness about her appearance severely narrowed her emotional and behavioural repertoire. I told her about Bentham's Panopticon (see p. 108), using it as an image of self-surveillance that has dangerous effects on women's ability to be themselves. I reframed 'complying with fashion dictates' as 'the prison of over-concern for appearance'. Marie said she was afraid to break out of this prison. I agreed that it was a difficult choice and posed the following dilemma – 'Should you continue to participate in your own imprisonment, feeling the safety of old ways, or should you make a break for it by daring to dress the way you please, wearing tighter clothes and defying the current fashion for slimness?' The look of fear in Marie's eyes was palpable, and she said she did not know.

She then abruptly changed the topic by saying that she had had a 'big fight' with her brother and mother during the week and had left home for a night, returning the next day. She felt that she had been picked on by her mother. During a fight with her brother, her mother had intervened to defend him. In response, I asked if she thought it was useful to have the whole family present in a session so that everyone could work in unison. She said she thought that would be a good idea and it meant she would have to tell her brother. I asked if this was a problem and if he was trustworthy. She said no to both questions and she agreed to ask the family to come to the next session.

In my message at the end of the session, I complimented Marie on the steps she had taken to reduce the bingeing and vomiting and commented on her determination. In setting tasks, I asked Marie to eat three meals a day, plus three snacks if she so desired; to use all the strategies that worked for her during the week to get on top of the bulimia; to initiate a conversation with a boy during the week; and to tell one other person about the bulimia.

Marie arrived first for our third session. The rest of the family were waiting in the car as they thought I would like to see her first. Marie told me she had a good week on the whole and that she was getting more on top of the bulimia. She binged twice on one day and the previous day she had had over-eaten rather than binged. I asked how she had managed to reduce the frequency of the bingeing and vomiting so much and she replied that continuing to do the things that worked for her were helping. She had told her brother, Lawrie, about the bulimia. He had surprised her by responding in a concerned way and then telling her she looked good in some clothes. Marie said that this was very different from what he had done before and that she felt much closer to him.

She asked me if initiating a conversation with a boy spontaneously counted as fulfilling one of the tasks assigned in the second session. I said she was clever and asked her how she had managed to complete the task so effortlessly. 'Just did it', was her reply.

Before the others came in, I asked Marie how they felt about coming. She replied that her mother was 'fine', her father did not see the point in coming at all and that her brother was confused and embarrassed. The family arrived and tentatively took their self-selected places in the room. Beverly and Marie sat close together on the couch and Ben, her father, sat to my right, his body turned away from me and his eyes studiously avoiding contact with mine. Lawrie sat further off still, looking slightly amazed by the proceedings. I began by explaining that Marie was taking some strides towards a more productive life, one 'without the tyranny of bulimia' and I felt that having the family attend this session would help that process along a little further.

I wanted at the outset of the session to encourage the family to focus on Marie's 'wins' and ways to make her 'win' more. This would ensure that the family would not inadvertently prolong the problem by not noticing and celebrating the signs of solution that had been generated so I asked if they had noticed any signs that Marie was moving past the bulimia. Beverly immediately said that she had noticed many: Marie was not taking as many showers since coming to see me; her face was not as swollen and her skin looked better; food she had bought now stayed in place in the pantry and did not mysteriously disappear.

I turned to the rest of the family and asked if anyone else had noticed any differences and Lawrie tentatively replied that Marie was not in such a bad mood. He immediately undercut the effect of this response by saying he and Marie were fighting 'a lot'. I externalised by asking, 'What effect has the fighting had on your relationship?'. Lawrie said that they were not talking, they mostly yelled at each other or hit out. Marie explained that they were once friends and she felt sad that they were now fighting so much. I asked, 'How will you know when things are going better for your relationship?' Marie said they would talk more. Lawrie agreed and said they would go out more together as they used to do. We spent some time discussing all the things they used to do together and the way in which they had once been good friends. I said perhaps these were the things they should look out for in the coming weeks.

Ben, Marie's father, was silent and occasionally restless during this conversation. I eventually turned to him and asked if he had noticed any differences in Marie, any signs that she was getting on top of the bulimia. He replied that Marie was wearing more individualistic clothes again. I asked if there was a different story about Marie, not the Marie victimised by pressure to conform to the standards of her peers in clothes and weight. Surprised at Ben's comment about her wearing more individualistic clothes I asked Marie if I could reveal to the family what we had spoken about in the last session. I asked 'Could you, the family, help me to catch up about this more individualistic and bold story about Marie?'

Beverly told me how self-determined Marie had been when she was younger and Ben endorsed this alternative, courageous description of Marie by saying how individual she had been. He looked out of the office window, stared at the blossoming magnolia tree, radiant on a spring morning, and remembered that Marie had liked an unusual and flamboyant skirt which she had worn until it virtually fell apart. Apparently no one could wrest the precious skirt from her.

I wondered out loud how Marie could reconnect to these old and bold ideas and how she could take these ideas and memories forward into the future. I asked the family who was least surprised to see Marie making some of her recent steps to separate from the bulimia. Ben quickly nominated himself and went on to say that he had always believed that Marie could do it. I asked what quality it was about Marie that led him to say this. He answered that it was the quality of determination. I asked, 'Is it the same quality that held on to the tattered skirt?' He said that he believed it was. I wondered out loud if that 'old bold quality' was now resurrecting in Marie.

I commented that this old bold story of Marie contrasted starkly with the impression created by Marie in our last session. This was an impression of someone imprisoned by peer group pressure and societal restraints about weight and appearance. I wondered how resurrecting the story of the 'old bold Marie' would strengthen her determination to defy societal prescriptions about how she should look and would give her permission to be herself. I hoped that the family's validation of this more deterministic Marie would encourage different patterns of interaction and perceptions of her and restrain family members from unhelpful behaviours in relation to her problem.

Marie seemed to be quietly taking all this in and then she abruptly spoke of her father's concern for her. Thinly veiling her sarcasm, she said she had not known that her father cared because when he was told about the bulimia, he sounded offended and then proceeded as though it had not happened. Beverly, as though ganging up on Ben, confirmed this.

Ben defensively replied that this was his way of coping. He reiterated that he also knew that she would get over the bulimia. I commented that he seemed very connected to this earlier story of Marie's 'boldness' – he was the first to mention it. The family then bluntly told me that Ben was often away and disconnected from the family. I asked if this was a problem. No one answered and Ben looked decidedly uncomfortable.

Beverly broke the silence by saying that she was over-connected and had caught herself taking too much of an interest on several occasions and had gone and done something else. However, on a few occasions when Marie wanted to talk to her she had made herself available. She said she felt so much better seeing the improvements in Marie and in herself. I asked if Marie had noticed and she said that she had. Beverly was being 'really good' and not questioning her which had helped her to deal with the bulimia alone and she felt this was better.

The thread of tension created by the question of Ben's absence from the family was still dangling. Beverly's face was impassive and Lawrie was looking out of the window, but Marie's angry look, not dispelled by the previous conversation, said it all. I turned to Ben and asked if there was anything he wanted to tell Marie. He said he really wanted Marie to know that he was there to talk to if she needed someone. She visibly softened, her face half hopeful in reply.

In my message at the end of the session I conveyed how impressed I was by Marie's courage and her solid determination to get on top of the problem, in particular the fact that she was not allowing herself to be a victim of the dictates of fashion and slimness. She had also allowed herself to be open to talking with Beverly – to 'talk up her feelings rather than eat over them'. I also mentioned how she and Lawrie were building up their relationship again as Marie released the stranglehold of the 'over-concern' for her appearance.

I said I was impressed by Beverly's ability to step back from the over-connection with Marie's problem. She seemed to be treading a difficult and very fine line between allowing Marie to solve her own problems and become her own person and yet still being there for her. I commented on Ben's offer of support for Marie – his saying he would be there for her when she wanted to talk. I was surprised at how quickly he had extended the invitation. I turned to Marie and asked, 'Was this a surprise for you?'. She said yes, and that she had not been aware of his support. I asked her whether, being aware of it, she would be more or less likely to offer Ben opportunities to talk with her. Marie said she would 'give it a go'.

I suggested once again that Marie was resurrecting the valuable parts of her old self. Also, it seemed that she had gained many strong qualities through her struggle with bulimia nervosa and I believed she would take these forward into the future and create a different and far more productive life.

At the close of the session I asked what was useful. Ben said that he was remembering more of the old story of Marie's determination and resolve. Beverly said she was surprised by Ben, learning that he was concerned and not 'flippant' about Marie's problems; implicitly she conveyed through this statement that she thought Ben's original response to the problem tried to deny its seriousness. I earmarked possible marital difficulties for later discussion. Lawrie did not know what was useful and Marie thought that 'everything' was useful. I asked if they were willing to come again and all said yes.

I commented that so many positive developments had happened for Marie that a celebration was probably in order. I asked whether they felt ready for a celebration to mark Marie's steps towards a new life. Beverly was really keen and they all joked about chocolate yogurts, saying that food was probably not a good thing to use for celebration.

Marie stayed behind after the family left and said that she had always had trouble with her father. I suggested that Marie and her father might like to come to see me together in the future. I also reminded her that relapses were normal when moving in a new direction and not to worry if she found herself giving in to the bulimia nervosa during stressful times. She could remember the ways in which she had defeated it and try those again.

Session four took place approximately four weeks later with Marie attending alone. She reported that everything was going well, she had not binged or vomited, and that she was feeling 'really good'. She related that the atmosphere at home was very tense, that her mother and father were fighting, and Beverly was very tense with the children. Marie told me that her brother had said that things were so bad at home he wanted to commit suicide. I suggested that she tell him he should speak with a counsellor.

Concerned that the home situation might mean a relapse for Marie, I posed a dilemma. I asked her whether she should take a step back from her parents' problems, just as Beverly had taken a step back from her over-concern with her bulimia (and allowed Marie to continue her own life and deal with her own problems), or whether she should step into her parents' marital life, attempting to solve their disputes and difficulties for them? She sat there, very still, silent and sad. I asked again, 'Should you step back from the unhappiness of your family life or should you step forwards towards self-care and independence?' Marie said she felt moving forwards was the right thing to do even though she felt bad about her parents' marriage. Even although it was hard to step back from the conflict between her mother and father, she thought it was the 'right thing to do' given the current level of her stress with exams and essays.

Marie volunteered that she was no longer interested in the boy she had spoken about earlier. She went on to explain that he was not interested in her and this did not bother her. Marie said she was 'feeling so much better'. She was by now having only two showers a day. She was still brushing her teeth three times a day and was now drinking milk and living on yogurt and cooked pasta and no longer eating dry pasta. I thought back to our first session when Marie so vividly explained that she could not eat these foods because they were 'horrible' to bring up again. She said that now if she thought about vomiting in the shower she immediately then thought, 'Why bother – it's disgusting'. She also said she overheard a classmate talking about bulimia. He scornfully tossed out 'that's for people sick in the head' and, in silent response, she felt very determined to defeat it. She said she thought that the bulimia did not control her weight so 'why should she keep on doing it?'.

She said the sessions encouraged Lawrie to see her in a 'very different way', and that this helped their relationship. She said that it was very different from before, that they were getting on well now. Beverly had stopped commenting about the bulimia and asking questions after our first session. Marie said this helped her to talk about the problem with her mother. This was 'different from how it was before'. She said this helped her to get over the bulimia since she was 'not worried' what mum was thinking.

At post-counselling on the Coopersmith Self-esteem Inventory, Marie was surprisingly still at pre-counselling levels, that is, the bottom 5 per cent on age-adjusted norms, but her scores on the Beck Depression Scale showed a marked improvement. She was now in the mildly depressed category. This was understandable, given the difficulties at home. Marie's scores on the Eating Disorders Inventory showed a marked decrease in all sub-scales except body dissatisfaction, in contrast with elevated scores on five sub-scales at pre-counselling. These improved scores accorded with Marie's increased sense of mastery over the bulimia nervosa and increased sense of satisfaction with her life.

Follow-up

I contacted Marie one month later and she said she was ready to end our sessions. 'Things are going fine,' she said. I offered support if she needed it in the future. Then we discussed the achievement of her goals. In response to the video questions I had asked Marie in our first session she replied that she was going out 'a lot more'. Before therapy, Marie had gone out once every two weeks. Now she was going out every Saturday night and whole weekends as well as during the week. I expressed concern that she might be overdoing it but she said she was enjoying herself. She was unperturbed: 'I am studying maybe four to five hours a week extra.' I asked her how she was managing to do so much extra work. She replied that previously the bulimia had taken up so much of her time that she now had more time for study.

I pointed out that the time immediately after giving up the bulimia was very difficult for many people, because they were then confronted by a great chasm of available time. Some people found it difficult to decide what to do with all that extra time. It was here that they were likely to fall victim to the bulimia again because it took away all these hard decisions by structuring their time for them. Marie replied that it was not difficult for her as her schoolwork was more than she could cope with. I commented that her schoolwork had in a sense become her ally in the battle against the bulimia. She agreed. As to her third goal of playing tennis she said she had not achieved this, as she was too busy studying.

Three months later I contacted Marie by phone for the long-term follow up. She reported that she had not binged or vomited since the last time we had spoken. In fact, she could not remember the last time she had done it. She had wanted to vomit three times in response to her parents' marital tension. Sometimes she had thought about vomiting in the shower but then thought, 'Why bother – it's just so disgusting'. She said she felt very determined to keep on top of the bulimia because it was not a good way to control her weight.

Marie's relationship with her brother had improved greatly. Now he gave her advice on her clothes and sometimes told her how good she looked. He also came into her room 'all the time', but without 'barging in' and going through her cupboards as he had done previously. He now asked before coming in. He was also following her around 'a lot lately'. She thought that breaking the secrecy surrounding the bulimia by letting him know about it had contributed a lot to the improvement in their relationship. Telling Lawrie had encouraged him to 'see me in a very different way' and had helped their relationship. They were getting along well now.

Marie also said her relationship with her father had improved. She volunteered an example. Marie had attracted an ardent young male admirer from her school – one that she did not want and could not dismiss. The admirer had come to her home and this had upset her. Her father told him to go home and then listened to Marie's concerns about the boy without denying or disqualifying her feelings. This was evidence for Marie that things had improved in her relationship with her father.

Marie said her relationship with her mother was still 'good'. Marie felt that her mother's questions and worried concern contributed to her guilt. After the first session, when Beverly had stopped questioning Marie about her bulimia, Marie began to tell Beverly about the bingeing and purging episodes, which made a beneficial difference to their relationship. Marie said that 'it enabled me to get over it [the bulimia] more quickly' and that she was not worried what Beverly was thinking. This helped her to feel much closer to Beverly.

Marie had once again completed the battery of tests. Her self-esteem score had risen at last to within the 45th percentile on age-adjusted norms. She was also approaching normality on the Beck Depression Scale, still, however, with a tendency to be mildly depressed. Her improved scores on all Eating Disorder Inventory sub-scales was maintained at this testing. It was clear from the collection of standardised information that Marie had improved in many areas of functioning. She agreed with this assessment.

She concluded by saying that talking with me had been very helpful. 'Breaking it [the bulimia] down' and 'analysing it more closely' helped her to see it 'more clearly'. Marie felt her confidence had improved as a result and now she reported wearing tighter fitting clothes and clothes which expressed her individuality. The old, bold Marie was back!

CHAPTER EIGHT

Case Study: Elizabeth

Elizabeth, a 20-year-old student of landscape design at a large university, told me in our first session that she binged and vomited an average of three to four times a day, excluding one day of the week. The day of exclusion was not a set day – it usually occurred when she was very busy with lectures, exams, small jobs and visits to her boyfriend and his family. When I asked how she had attempted to defeat the problem prior to seeing me, she said that direct attempts to reduce the vomiting and bingeing had not worked. Keeping her time well-planned and highly structured with lectures, exams, small jobs and visits had sometimes worked, simply because Elizabeth did not have the time to binge and purge. She was too busy with university demands and social activities.

The bingeing and purging had begun six years previously following an attempt to diet. She said that vomiting was the easy solution to bingeing and not putting on weight. These behaviours began infrequently at first, then, over a two-year period, gradually increased in frequency until they reached the current levels. It was interesting that, two years previously, Elizabeth travelled overseas – she said she was happy for the entire period and she did not binge or vomit. She said she was more herself as she did not care what people thought of her, since she probably would not see them again.

Elizabeth had received counselling ten years previously for a period of two months. She said her parents forced her to attend these sessions but that she was too shy really to get anything out of them. Her second attempt at counselling occurred while attending

university; she went to counselling sessions at the university counselling centre. She had two counsellors during a five-month period; the
first, according to Elizabeth, predominantly used relaxation training
which Elizabeth did not find very useful, and the second counsellor
used a family therapy approach trying to 'find who was at fault'.
Elizabeth said she did not think any of her family were to blame for
her bulimia and stopped seeing the counsellor. She said that neither
of these attempts to reduce the problem helped because the counsellors' main focus was to reduce the bingeing and purging and
Elizabeth could not do so. In Elizabeth's own words, she was waiting
for 'a miracle cure' – she was rigid and immobile as she told me this,
her face like a mask and her hands held stiffly over her stomach. She
knew that a miracle cure was irrational, and that she would have to do
something to help herself.

Baseline data had been collected after the initial phone call and in
the intervening period (two weeks) before the first counselling
session. Elizabeth's pre-counselling rating on the Coopersmith
Self-esteem Inventory placed her extremely low, in the bottom 1 per
cent. These paper and pencil self-reports correlated with Elizabeth's
verbal self-reports and my clinical impressions at this first session.
Elizabeth's pre-counselling score on the Beck Depression Scale
placed her in the severely depressed category. This finding correlated
with her own verbal reports of depressed mood, a diminished
pleasure in her usual activities, fatigue and a sense of worthlessness
and suicidal depression. She showed elevated scores on the Eating
Disorders Inventory on all sub-scales except perfectionism. Her
highest scores were on the ineffectiveness and interoceptive awareness subscales. Ineffectiveness assesses feelings of general inadequacy,
insecurity, worthlessness, and the feeling of not being in control of
one's life. Interoceptive awareness indicates a lack of confidence in
recognising and accurately identifying emotions or visceral
sensations of hunger or satiety. I showed these results to Elizabeth
and she thought they were a good reflection of her current state. (See
Appendix for explanation of these tests.)

In the next session, as in subsequent sessions, I collected Elizabeth's data on the frequency of bingeing and vomiting from the previous week. In this session, the frequency of the behaviours remained the same. I searched for exceptions to the problem by asking how she had managed to stay the same. Her answer was that, by keeping busy, she did not think about bingeing or purging. Then she told me that she usually ate breakfast every morning. I was curious about how she was able to have a routine over breakfast. Elizabeth said she often found it difficult to have any routine so, commenting on her ability to have a discrete meal, I said that this was a helpful step to getting better and that she did seem to have some control over her food intake, which was a good sign.

We then considered her goals for therapy, and I asked, 'How will you know when the problem is solved?'. When she had trouble answering this question, I asked her, 'If I were to make a video of you when everything was fine and you were over the problem, what would be happening in the video?'. Elizabeth listed a number of goals. The first was that she would no longer binge and vomit. When asked what she would be doing in the place of these activities, she said she would try healthier behaviours. She elaborated by saying that she saw herself as having breakfast, lunch and dinner, and not worrying if she had anything extra. She also thought she would be doing much better with her university studies, particularly in being more organised and not procrastinating. Most of all Elizabeth wanted to be happy, to get up in the morning, thinking enthusiastically about what she would be doing during the day. Her energy levels would be high and she would care about life, having fun instead of being moody. She said she would have more fun with friends, especially with friends other than her boyfriend's friends. She particularly wanted to play sport such as non-competitive hockey and indoor cricket.

In the third session, Elizabeth spoke about one of the main obstacles to achieving her goals – her disorganisation. She worried about what others thought of her disorganisation and it made her feel guilty which, in turn, encouraged more worry. She also said she would swing between worrying too much and not caring at all about her life. When asked about times when she did not worry but also cared, she easily cited three occasions – in primary school, with her boyfriend and during her overseas trip. I attempted to explore the qualities she had that encouraged caring about life without worrying. However, she wanted to explore the obstacles.

Elizabeth said she attached undue importance to others' opinions of herself, giving them a reality, even if they were not true. She then told of an incident with one of her bosses, who said to her that she was unreliable for coming to work late even though she had previously told her other boss that she would be late. The first boss apologised later, but Elizabeth reported feeling 'really bad' for quite a while after the event. She said that she believed the shameful feelings she felt, rather than the facts of the situation. Elizabeth said that she believed that other people's perceptions of her were more valid than her own. If others spoke to her in a deprecating or critical manner, she would subject herself to intense self-punishment, even when she knew or believed their opinions to be untrue.

I asked her what, if her boyfriend had been there during or after the incident, he would have said about the boss who condemned her? She said he would say, 'It was rubbish'. I asked her what her mother would have said about the incident, if she had been there: 'She would say, take it with a grain of salt.' Given these opinions from people she respected and loved, I wondered how she could temper what she told herself in unfair situations such as these. She immediately said 'by thinking about others' perspectives'. I also wondered out loud whether her shame sometimes prevented her from feeling angry at unfair criticism; whether she somehow turned the anger in on herself rather than constructively directing it outward. I asked if expressing disapproval or anger was a problem for her. Elizabeth looked genuinely puzzled and did not reply, steadily gazing at me.

In my message at the end of session three, I complimented Elizabeth on continuing the pattern of not bingeing at all on one day.

Even though this was her usual pattern, it was still an achievement when she was attempting to change a number of unhelpful patterns in her life. I suggested that a busy structured day seemed to be an 'ally' against the vomiting and bingeing. I also said that, given her progress, it was better for us to be like two scientists, simply observing the pattern of the frequency of the bingeing and vomiting. For this reason, she should stay the same and not try to alter the frequency by reducing it. I asked her to notice what happened on days when she had a fixed routine and was busy. She suggested that she would like to keep really busy on the second day after she normally did not binge or purge – not bingeing or purging on the second day would break the pattern. She said university demands alone would keep her very busy so she should have no trouble fulfilling this aspect of the task.

At the beginning of the fourth session, Elizabeth said she was feeling 'hopeful' about being 'normal' – the frequency of bingeing and vomiting behaviour had decreased to once daily in the intervening week. She was speaking in a much more animated fashion, drawing her hands away from her stomach for most of the conversation and using them to emphasise a point. When I commented that she had managed to make it only once daily, and this was an excellent step forward, she opened her hands again and said she did it 'by keeping busy'.

Elizabeth brought up for discussion the subject of her lack of self-confidence. This was only after some prompting, however, as when asked what she wanted to talk about, she often said she did not know. I would ask, 'Who would know?' and use circular questions about friends, family and her boyfriend in order to find a lead into the session. What would her boyfriend suggest as a good topic to talk about (or her mother or friends)? Eventually, she replied that her friends would say that she had no self-confidence. Elizabeth then said that her lack of self-confidence was her biggest problem.

I asked her what would be the first sign in her life that she had developed self-confidence. She quickly replied that she would not be too scared to ask questions or offer comments during tutorials. We explored her difficulty in speaking during tutorials. I asked Elizabeth to scale her frequency of speaking from one to ten, with one, representing not speaking at all and ten, speaking most of everyone in the tutorial. She said she was at a one, where she did not speak at all, and she would like to be at a five, speaking occasionally. I asked what effect the fear of speaking during tutorials had on her self-confidence and I helped her to search for ways in which she had stood up to the fear. We also explored the effect that more frequent speaking would have on her levels of self-confidence, the quality of her current work, and her future career. I suggested that speaking in tutorials was one small step she could take to become more self-confident, competent and satisfied with her education.

Elizabeth said it was her concern for what others thought about her that got in the way of her satisfaction. She was too worried about others' opinions to notice the quality of education she was receiving. I asked Elizabeth whether there were times when she did not worry so much about others' opinions, and she said she did not worry if she did not like the other person. I asked, 'How do you manage to not worry with people you do not like?' Elizabeth elaborated: she did not worry if the people with whom she was interacting were ' horrible people who were rude' or if she didn't like the look of them, or if she didn't like what they did or their personality. I was curious about how plenty of self-confidence would help her in these situations. Elizabeth said she would probably judge people less and compare herself to others less. She would not need her criteria for disregarding worry at all. She would be so filled with self-confidence that she would behave in the same way to everyone.

I asked if she often compared herself to others. In response, Elizabeth nodded and drew a distinction between 'good' and 'bad' competition. If she could do something about the competition, that is, learn from it, then it was 'good' competition; if she could not do anything about it then it was 'bad' competition. She felt that she often indulged in 'bad' competition.

I asked Elizabeth, 'If, over the next few months, you deliberately make 'good' competition a feature of your interactions with others, what differences would you notice in your life?' Elizabeth replied that she would not be worrying about the things she could not change, and she would be learning a lot more from others. I then asked, 'What would be the first sign that you are using these competitive feelings as an opportunity to improve your skills?' Elizabeth said, 'Going and doing something about it,' which she did immediately after our session.

In my message at the end of this session, I complimented Elizabeth on bingeing and vomiting much less, and not at all on one day during the previous week. I said that she had taken strong steps toward getting on top of the bingeing and vomiting, but I cautioned that she might be moving too fast and that maybe we needed to slow down. She said this was definitely not the case. I also suggested that she might like to change other aspects of her life apart from the bulimic behaviour so that she was advancing on a number of fronts. I suggested that she speak up in tutorials in the coming week and observe the effect it had on her levels of self-confidence and on her perception of the opinions of others. I also suggested that she experiment with any competitive or jealous twinges and use them as opportunities to develop herself. Elizabeth said she would immediately go down and look at a painting by a classmate (of whom she had been jealous) to see the techniques he employed.

The fifth session could be aptly subtitled 'Making mountains out of cardboard'. Elizabeth reported that the task of using competitive feelings as a spur to action was 'a really good thing to be doing'. She reported that, after our session, she went and looked at the classmate's paintings and learnt a great deal. Previously, she would have just felt jealous and become upset with herself, bingeing and purging more often immediately after the incident. Elizabeth also reported that she used this approach of 'good competition' with three other assignments, one of which involved making mountains out of cardboard for a design project. She watched other people and learnt from their techniques. I asked her what quality in her transmuted jealous feelings into productive feelings. We explored flexibility and her willingness to be open to new experience.

Elizabeth reported that the second task turned out to be a 'disaster'. For the first time, she had spoken up in her tutorial. She said the lecturer was very arrogant and critical of all comments, except those paraphrasing his own opinions. She said she only got halfway through her comment and then 'collapsed in a heap'. She had actually spoken up for the first time in a difficult tutorial and managed to utter a coherent comment. The tutor had cut her comment off but at least she had got halfway. She said her classmates need not have known that she was only halfway. I asked her how she had managed to defy the feelings of embarrassment and still speak up. She said that she did not know. The first part of this session was spent 'transmuting' the disaster into a partial success. I asked how she had managed to get halfway. She said that she did not think about what she was going to say in the tutorial. I said, 'When you don't get in your own way, you can at least get halfway' and we both laughed. I asked, 'When you get the full way, what will you be doing differently?' She said saying what she wanted to say until the end. 'What would you need to be doing differently to get to the end?' I asked. 'Probably persisting despite what anyone else does', she replied.

I then went on, 'If I were to ask the participants, "How silly was Elizabeth's comment?" and they rated you along a continuum where one is not silly at all and ten is stupidly outrageous, where would they place you?' Elizabeth said a five. I asked how she would rate her classmates' comments. She replied, a five also. I commented that if both were a five, then she rated favourably against them. She said she still felt awful. I asked if she valued the tutor's opinion and she said she did not; she found him boorish and arrogant. I reminded her that she had told me that she could be more confident if she felt the other person was horrible, and even though she ultimately wanted to feel confident with everyone despite their likeability, this thought could help her to persist in speaking up in his tutorials. Elizabeth said her tutor would probably rate everyone at a 12. When I asked Elizabeth what she thought her next step should be, she said maybe saying a couple of things half-way or one thing the whole way. Later in the interview, she decided to concentrate on one thing the whole way.

I asked, 'If you were ten years down the track and were more self-confident, what would you be advising yourself to do to get on top of the self-confidence problem?' She replied, 'Just saying what you think'. We then explored the effect of speaking up versus not speaking up. Elizabeth said that she would get more out of everything if she spoke up, that she would talk 'more freely to everyone and feel more confident'. She would also clear up misunderstandings. If she did not speak up, she would 'miss out on a lot and wouldn't get much out of anything'.

We then turned to the bingeing and vomiting because Elizabeth expressed some confusion about what to change first – that, or the rest of her life. We examined the effect of starting with either. When asked, 'What effect did changing the bingeing and purging have on you?', she said it had an immediate good effect. I asked about the effect of changing her behaviour in tutorials and when she felt jealous and Elizabeth responded that it was 'not so good an effect'. With reducing the bingeing and vomiting she felt much more confident but with changing aspects of the rest of her life, she sometimes felt embarrassed and binged and ate more in response. Elizabeth decided we should concentrate on reducing the bingeing and vomiting but not to the exclusion of the rest of her life.

I asked her whether, if she had three meals a day, she would be more or less likely to binge. Elizabeth replied, 'Less likely.' However, she was concerned that if she began to eat three meals a day she would feel full, and 'that's what sets me off'. The feeling of fullness was acting as a trigger to bouts of bingeing and vomiting. I searched for exceptions to this: 'Have you ever defied the perception that being full is somehow wrong and allowed yourself to feel full without going on to bingeing and purging?' Elizabeth replied that she found this very difficult. I asked her what, if she could defy this perception, she would be doing instead of bingeing and purging? She said she would continue with her normal activities. She said she would often wake up on Tuesday morning after a day without bingeing and purging and feel 'very bad', often not attending lectures. She would then binge and vomit with increased frequency. I suggested that on Tuesday morning she should defy the perception that 'full is bad' by attending lectures. I asked her how confident she felt about doing this. Elizabeth said she felt far more confident because she was telling me. She also said she would tell her boyfriend about it and they could celebrate the breaking up of an old pattern.

At the end of the session, I said I was impressed by Elizabeth's ability to reduce the bingeing and purging. I reiterated that she was unsure whether to work directly with the bingeing and vomiting or whether to work indirectly with the rest of her life. Even though she had success with working with the rest of her life, this did not seem to reduce the bingeing and purging. I suggested that we try to experiment with dealing with the bingeing and vomiting more directly. I asked Elizabeth to build on the Mondays when she did not binge and vomit; that is, she was asked to extend the problem-free time from the customary one day to two days. I also asked her to add three meals a day. We had discussed how Elizabeth could defy the feelings of guilt that would arise from eating three meals a day, and these were reiterated as well as the ways in which she could defy the perception that it was wrong to have feelings of fullness following a meal. Such feelings need not act as a trigger to bouts of bingeing and vomiting.

Elizabeth said that that session was 'really good'. She got clear in her mind about many things that were previously 'confusing'. She also felt it was useful to sum up as it helped her to categorise everything. She found sorting out what should have the most emphasis – bingeing/purging or 'the rest of her life' – gave her hope that she would 'get on top of the problem'. She said she was feeling more confident in herself and feeling more hopeful about her life. Although she still felt moody, she was beginning to think more about her life and how she could contribute to her own happiness.

Session six was extremely short as Elizabeth was in the middle of exams and essays and could not concentrate. She said she wanted to meet when the essays and exam period were finished. Elizabeth was feeling good about having broken the pattern of bingeing and purging on her second day. She had not binged or purged at all on the previous Tuesday, meaning that she was problem-free for two days of the week instead of one. She had also had three meals a day for most of the week. We explored the effect of going without bingeing and purging for six months. Elizabeth thought she would enjoy things a lot more, she would not get grumpy, she would speak up despite her feelings of shyness, she would play sport and she would be healthy. I suggested that the bingeing and vomiting was 'eating up your time'. Elizabeth spontaneously contrasted this with 'having more time to do things' if she continued this new life. We contrasted the effects of a life of 'having more time' as opposed to a life where bingeing and vomiting 'eats up the time'.

Elizabeth said she wanted to talk about being more organised with her work. When asked, 'What stops you from being organised?', she replied that the vomiting and bingeing made her disorganised by cutting down her time. We discussed family attitudes to her being disorganised, but Elizabeth was adamant throughout counselling that her parents were not responsible for any of her predicaments.

It became clear as we talked that Elizabeth was very concerned about failing nearly everything she tried. She even liked to hand in essays without any contact with the tutor or lecturer because she was afraid he might tell her that she had failed. When asked to consider the habits fear of failure had coached in her, she said she would not consider asking a lecturer to offer some guidance about an essay, for example. I asked what effect this approach might have on the quality of her work, and she replied that it made her grade on the essay a matter of 'pot luck'. I asked how she could turn 'pot luck' into a 'certainty' and she replied that going and talking to the lecturer, despite her fears, would make it heaps better.

In the task at the end of the session she was asked to continue to go without bingeing and vomiting for two full days, and to continue to have three meals a day. Elizabeth was asked to notice what effect going without bingeing and purging had on the way she organised her time.

Session seven was one month later. Time between sessions had varied according to Elizabeth's hectic university schedule – it had averaged out to one to two weeks between sessions except for the university semester break where I saw Elizabeth once a month for two months. Elizabeth reported that she had returned to vomiting and bingeing two to three times a day and that although initially she had started to move forward, she now felt she had taken some steps backward. She felt the university holidays had been bad for her in that she had binged and vomited more. I wondered if it had been unwise to leave so much time between sessions, particularly when she had more time on her hands, was stressed by examinations, and we were trying to change the bingeing and purging so directly.

She also reported feeling tired all the time, and that her flatmate had glandular fever. She said she felt stuck. I said I felt genuinely perplexed – the bulimia was resisting us and I did not know why. I also admitted that I felt defeated by some of Elizabeth's attitudes about her weight. Elizabeth immediately responded by talking about some of the 'good' effects of our sessions. She felt that it was good to give her the 'planned binge' task because even though she would binge it would mean that she was controlling it still. Elizabeth also said that as a result of coming to sessions she was 'thinking more positively about things and not worrying so much'. She said she was speaking up more about her feelings. She said that the sessions had made her think more about what she was doing. She said she felt better, with much more of a positive attitude.

Elizabeth then wanted to discuss some of the attitudes that caused problems for her. She said she felt ugly in comparison to others. I told her about Bentham's Panopticon – an eighteenth century prison designed by Bentham that would require no wardens as it was in effect self-policing. I said that keeping a vigilant and critical eye on oneself was tantamount to keeping oneself in a prison. Escaping meant that she could deviate from the current pencil-thin ideal body type. Elizabeth said, 'That's how it feels, that's what it is like.' I asked, 'What would you need to do to open the door of the prison and walk outside?' She said, 'Not worry about what others think,' and that she always wanted to be 'the best'. We discussed the changes she had already made and how they had allowed her to step outside the prison of over-concern for what others thought about her. I also said that, because the security arrangements in the prison were so subtle, she was probably going to persist in self-policing for some time, and that was why she needed to keep challenging the self-policing by attempting new tasks even though she may feel that she was not moving forward.

This session was very short as Elizabeth was in the middle of examination time, her most stressful time at university. If she had managed to maintain the period without bingeing and vomiting for two days, I probably would have extended it to three days. However, this had not worked so I asked Elizabeth to have a planned binge. She said she thought it was important to determine unconscious reasons motivating her behaviour, so I asked her to examine the thoughts and feelings about having this planned binge in an attempt to find out why she was finding it difficult to reduce the frequency of bingeing and vomiting. Also, this task would not be too stressful as she would probably have a binge anyway, so she might as well turn it into a useful one. In my message at the end of the session, I began by using the metaphor of a 'life raft' – was she ready to leave the security of the life raft and swim to shore, to risk the waves that would probably come crashing down on her head? She said, 'I am, but I cling to everything. I hang on as long as I can. I really want to but I don't know how to.' I asked, 'What would be the effect of clinging on for another six months – would it make you more ready or 'less ready' to hang on?' (collapsing the future). She replied less ready and that when she went to see her first counsellor when she first got bulimia, the counsellor said she was not ready. When would she ever be ready? she said despondently.

Elizabeth said again that she wanted to let go – it was a case of 'sink or swim'. I stressed that each little bit would help, and that each time something did not work, that would be a useful hint either to do something different or to try in a different way. I also reminded her that she had had the problem for a long time; it would take some time to defeat it. I then asked her to do three things:

1. go to a doctor she could trust (I mentioned a couple of general practitioners who were informed and sympathetic about the problem), tell them that she had bulimia nervosa and ask for a full medical check-up (Elizabeth was complaining about great tiredness and had expressed several times that she was worried about the effect of the bulimia on her health. I suggested she would have a clear mind about possible medical complications of bulimia if she had a check-up)

2. defy the bulimia by having three meals a day

3. vomit before bingeing, to gently break up the habit, which had grown very hard and cold; she needed to stir it up to change it (I gained Elizabeth's blind agreement before I told her this last task.)

Elizabeth discontinued counselling after this session, saying that she had reduced the frequency of bingeing and purging as much as she wanted to at this point. There was too much stress from her university work to continue.

When I rang her after a month she told me her bingeing and vomiting behaviour was reduced by nearly a half. She was bingeing and vomiting one to two times a day as opposed to the three to four times when she first started. She also occasionally went without vomiting and bingeing for up to three days. She commented that although she had not achieved complete cessation of all vomiting and bingeing, she felt she had taken some considerable steps towards achieving her goal, and she realised it would be a slow process for her.

I suggested that when life was not so stressful for her, she might like to come back. I also recommended other therapists that she could see if she felt we could no longer work productively. She said she felt very comfortable with me and that she would return. I then asked about progress on her other goals.

She said she was much healthier – she now rode her bike around the city's lake every day and she enjoyed this very much. She said she was eating three meals a day but she still worried if she had anything extra. She also reported that she was now able to recognise when she was procrastinating and to choose to do so or not. She said this was very different from before when she did not know if she was procrastinating. Elizabeth reported that she felt more relaxed and a 'bit happier' but not as happy as she would have liked. She said she was still fairly moody. Her energy levels were a 'bit better', likewise her caring about life. She had begun hockey in the previous semester but found this commitment along with her studies too difficult to keep. Her bike riding was enough for the moment.

She said she still did not have separate friends from her boyfriend's friends. She still felt fairly shy and did not know how to begin conversations. I asked how she felt about herself, as this is what Elizabeth described as one of her major problems. She replied that before, her self-confidence was 'really bad' all the time, and now it was a mixture of 'really good', 'very bad' and 'all right'. Predominantly, it was 'all right'. She often felt 'bad' around confident people and 'jealousy' was still a problem for her but 'not as much of a problem as before'. She could now occasionally let people have their special abilities and feel that she had something special to contribute too.

At long term follow-up, three months later, Elizabeth said that she was still bingeing and vomiting but that its frequency had reduced to about half that of the baseline period, that is, it had reduced to one to two times daily, and that occasionally she was still going without bingeing and vomiting for up to three days. She felt that she was slowly improving. She was having breakfast, lunch and dinner most days but she still worried if she had anything extra. She said she was a little more organised – she had a book to write in her tasks for the day and that this had helped. She reported that she still had 'ups and downs' but that, for many months, she had been able to talk herself around and become happy again. She said she was not as moody as she used to be and that she was more able to have fun rather than worrying about what other people thought. She said she did not have as many friends as she would like but that she was having more fun with friends. She said she had no time to pursue sport. In addition, she said she was spending more time with people and that this 'just seemed to happen'.

Elizabeth's scores on the Coopersmith Self-esteem Inventory improved slightly at post-counselling but by long-term follow-up, three months later, they had returned to pre-counselling levels. Her score on the Beck Depression Scale placed her in the mildly to moderately depressed category at post-counselling, an improvement from the severely depressed category at pre-counselling. At long-term follow-up, she was categorised on this inventory, once again, as severely depressed. At post-counselling on the Eating Disorder Inventory, there was an improvement in all sub-scales. This may have reflected Elizabeth's reported increased sense of control over her eating behaviour and health. At long-term follow-up, sub-scale scores improved from pre-counselling level on the following subscales: bulimia, ineffectiveness, interpersonal distrust, interoceptive awareness and maturity fears. Sub-scale scores rose to elevated pre-test levels on drive for thinness and body dissatisfaction.

Elizabeth had reduced the bulimic behaviour by half and had taken some steps towards achieving four of her seven goals. However, her long history of bulimic behaviour and the stability of the frequency and severity of bingeing and purging behaviour suggested that she still needed assistance to eliminate the problem.

CHAPTER NINE

Control as the Central Theme

In this chapter, I show the centrality of the issue of control for working effectively with clients with bulimia nervosa. I define the issue (and associated concepts) within the therapeutic context, showing its importance in the case studies and exploring its significance for effective therapy. I also show why therapists are uncomfortable with the issues of power and control to the extent that these issues are under-emphasised in training, research and the general family therapy literature. The feminist debate on the political aspects of power has much to contribute to our understanding of power and control, and I therefore examine the debate within the therapeutic context. I also list the specific therapeutic practices that avoid control of the therapeutic process by the therapist and that allow the client to assume increasing control over her own life.

Power and control

The case studies – Susanne, Marie and Elizabeth, together with the client's report presented in the foreword to this book – show in differing emphases the need for an understanding of control in addressing the four themes of bulimia nervosa – behavioural, interpersonal, developmental and sociocultural. They particularly show the importance of the sociocultural factors in producing and maintaining a sense of loss of personal control. There were strong sociocultural factors in Susanne's troubled relationships, Marie's family tensions and her need to conform to the societal dictates of beauty and fashion, Elizabeth's comparisons with others, and the client's destructive study and work experience.

Each individual experienced a lack of control in these contexts and, accordingly, exacted control over her own body as a way of handling the tensions. She also attempted to control the intrapersonal domain – for example, Susanne's distress at her 'too wild feelings', or Elizabeth's self-punishment for undeserved criticism; and also she tried to control the interpersonal domain – for example, Marie's regulation of her mother's attempts to control the problem.

The control that was attempted to redress the 'out of control' feeling ended up, ironically, making the client more 'out of control' than ever. Any attempt by others, including the therapist, to take control of the problem also resulted in the same outcome. In all cases, I needed to discourage others in the client's life from taking control of the problem, and to avoid taking control of the problem myself, so that the client could gain a sense of sovereignty over her life. The therapist, in particular, must use all her persuasive powers to influence rather than control otherwise she will fall into the well-entrenched patterns and outcomes of other relationships in the client's life. He or she must avoid becoming locked in the client's subtle attempts inappropriately and unconsciously to control others and events, actions the client initiates in order to deal with her own distress.

How can we consciously and effectively work with the issue of control in the therapeutic process, rather than unwittingly becoming locked in a escalation of wills? An important step in increasing our effectiveness with bulimic clients is to address this question. To work *with* rather than *against* the client, therapists need to come to terms with a cluster of concepts, namely power, control, manipulation and influence. The following definitions attempt to draw distinctions between these concepts,

> *Power* is the 'ability to effect tangible outcomes whether that power is achieved through the accumulation of money, property, muscles, beauty or knowledge and whether the effect is for self or others' (Langer 1983, p.15)

Control is the 'active belief that one has a choice among responses that are differentially effective in achieving the desired outcome' (Langer 1983, p.20).

Manipulation is the 'artful and devious management of people or events' (Macquarie Dictionary).

Influence is 'the movement towards a desired action by an invisible power' (Macquarie Dictionary).

According to these definitions, power is the actual ability to effect changes in the world and control is the perception of that ability. Manipulation is an underhand way of expressing power, that is, of effecting changes in the world and influence is a direct encouragement of action that is not sanctioned by power.

There is a recursive relationship between the self and the larger world's social system that needs to be honoured in therapy – that is, the therapist must respect and work with the interplay between the individual in the system and the system in the individual. From both the systemic and feminist perspectives, the addictive pattern of bingeing and purging is a microcosmic process reflecting the imbalances of power in the larger social context; (Lobsinger 1997). The client's lack of self-control will be reflected in her perceived lack of power in the larger society and social inequities will be reflected in her sense of personal powerlessness. The individual unsuccessfully attempts to control her own experience within an oppressive relational context, where she also feels little control.

The client's 'power over' events or persons is an illusory form of control. The power over weight dissatisfaction, through bingeing and purging, is misplaced, quickly growing out of control when the problem becomes addictive. The 'power over' others to change their behaviour can swing into manipulative struggles that are unproductive and time consuming. When the client begins to take control of her life rather than her weight, she can move to a position of 'power to achieve' certain outcomes. Her capacity to be honest and assertive with others will encourage greater intimacy. The therapist needs to assist the client to change her perception so that she takes the power to achieve certain outcomes.

While control over the frequency of bingeing and purging and control over the psychological dynamic embedded in the problem are the most obvious areas for the cultivation of a sense of direct influence by the client, encouraging a sense of control in the interpersonal and sociocultural domains also seems necessary to increase her sense of power in the wider sphere. In the interpersonal world of the client it is necessary to encourage her to assume greater power to take risks in her behaviour, thoughts, attitudes and beliefs. Greater risk-taking behaviour in relation to others ultimately fosters a feeling of command or authorship over life which is often at odds with the wishes of friends, family or lovers. The client will need many skills for dealing with the fall-out from more assertive behaviour.

It may also be necessary, for example, to encourage the client's sense of power by challenging societal female prescriptions of femininity where it is dogged by compliance and agreeability, and to argue against the indirect or 'inappropriate expression of emotion' and the internalised societal prescription of the 'thin ideal' (often at variance with the client's body shape). Encouraging the client to be defiant, whether this is a private or public act, assists in the process of healing. Therapists will facilitate this process if they encourage 'give and take' in terms of control over the sessions and the determination of tasks and goals.

Before addressing the ways in which I attempt to influence without controlling, it is necessary to locate therapeutic ideas of control in an historical context and also to cite the continuing debate on this issue by feminists. Many therapists, limited by their theoretical adherence, are uncomfortable with notions of their own or their clients' power in the world, and prefer to avoid these sociopolitical aspects of therapy. Realising the way in which theory has been formed over time by specific individuals helps us to examine the perception that its assumptions are inviolable. The feminist perspective offers a useful lens for examining these assumptions. It helps us to see the political and social ramifications of therapeutic practices arising from these assumptions and to examine their desirability for social justice and equity. The following section explains the way in which theoretical frameworks in family therapy, in particular, have impeded therapists' understanding of power and control and uses the lens of feminism to examine its desirability.

The historical and political context

Gregory Bateson, one of the most influential contributors to the field of psychology and certainly that of family therapy, wrote persuasively on this subject. It is from him that the field of family therapy has derived a contentious understanding of power. Bateson (1979) rejected the notion of power and his objection centred around two notions. In the first notion, Bateson saw power as an epistemological error. He proposed that power, as a unilateral concept, does not account for the notion of recursiveness which was central to systemic approaches. This notion states that one individual cannot be the cause or effect of another's actions. In a circular world and from a certain distance, each is acting and acted upon simultaneously. Each plays a part in a holistic pattern.

Bateson's second notion is perhaps even more contentious. He posited that the description of human events based on power was inherently 'toxic' – for example, the ecological repercussions of our interference (power) with the environment provides a case in testimony for the notion of recursiveness. Within the human sphere, causal ascription to a party or event for a problem is inaccurate and dangerous. All parties mutually play a role in developing and maintaining the problem.

As a result of Bateson's implicit censorship of discourse on power, very little was written on power in systemic literature. This stands in sharp contrast to the discourse on power in ideological movements, such as Marxism and feminism of the 1960s and 1970s, the period in which family therapy was burgeoning (Flaskas 1990).

There were therapists within family therapy who disagreed with Bateson's analysis. Haley (1976) argued against Bateson's dismissal of power and two separate streams of therapy evolved on this issue. Several theorists have mirrored Bateson's assumptions by minimising power issues, preferring to see therapy as a kind of conversation (Andersen and Goolishian 1988) with implications of equal power within that relationship.

Other theorists argued that not naming power is in itself more 'toxic'. For example, not naming power in domestic violence may rationalise abusive actions by implying the victim is recursively reacting to the perpetrator. Feminists within this tradition (Flaskas 1990; McGregor 1990) were alarmed by the implications of recursiveness within the politically sensitive areas of sexual abuse and domestic violence. They argued that power should be placed on the political and theoretical agenda of family therapy.

More recent feminists (Lohyn 1994; Wolf 1993) have argued that the sociopolitical context is now sufficiently different for women to claim legitimate power in society and that women need to move from the position of 'victim' feminism. They say that there is a distinction between victim feminism and power feminism. Victim feminism creates a dualism between personal power (over one's body and personal life) and public power (the use of money and influence to make changes for other women). The former is acceptable, while the latter is seen as taking power from others. The rejection of victim feminism, of course, does not account for those women who do not have money or influence and are unlikely to obtain them, although some feminists think that oppressed women can still be powerful by refusing to accept definitions of them that are put forward by the powerful (Lohyn 1994). They can move blame and criticism away from themselves to decision makers who are responsible for the injustices they experience.

Other therapists from family therapy (White and Epston 1989) have used alternative lenses to deconstruct power within therapy. They have turned towards Foucault and Constructivism for discourse on power. Foucault (1984) comments on the notion of power, its productive force (its positive potential in the creation of discourse) and its relational nature; that is, it exists in interpersonal relationships. Foucault sites power in specific contexts and says it invokes the notion of resistance. White (1989) has appropriated ideas from Foucault and incorporated them into his theoretical orientation in the following way. White sees power as positive and creative in its effects. He speculates that intimate relationships are made between power and knowledge and that power becomes evident in the practices that surround people. He also speculates that dominant knowledges become all-powerful and alternative knowledges become marginalised. White's therapeutic practice of restoring alternative knowledge makes much sense in the context of these ideas.

Influence in therapy

How can therapists influence clients within the context of these ideas? Many practitioners and theorists actively avoid controlling the therapeutic process when working with anorexic and bulimic clients (Bruch 1978; Madanes, 1981; Selvini-Palazzoli *et al.* 1978). They realise that there is no power to struggle for (McFarland 1997).

Selvini-Palazzoli (Selvini-Palazzoli *et al.* 1978) was one of the first therapists to stress the need to avoid control games between therapist and client. The first step in avoiding control games was for the therapist to interpret the client's 'resistance' of the system as a way of maintaining the status quo. The client may believe that she is protecting the cohesion and well-being of the system (McFarland 1997; Selvini-Palazzoli *et al.* 1978). This approach serves to initiate common ground, where both therapist and client can work on building collaboration, furthering self-awareness and goal setting (McFarland 1997). For example, Susanne's feral feelings were the triggers to a binge and purge but also functioned as helpful reminders of her own feelings when she was in danger of forgetting her needs. Further, bingeing and purging could be interpreted as a sign that she was forgetting to nurture herself, and she could use this sign to redirect her actions and increase her agency in her life. If the symptom is framed as a protective mechanism for the client, and reinforced by the therapist when she actually restrains change (that is, cites the negative effects of any change), the client might be encouraged to realise that it is she who controls and restrains progress, and not the therapist. It is her sense of agency that will ultimately abandon the symptom, not the motivation of the therapist. Once this realisation occurs, the therapist is released from a position 'which implicitly urges the patient to change or to relinquish the resistant posture' (Lerner and Lerner 1983, p.395).

The second step in avoiding such games was to realise that the need to control could potentially symmetrically escalate for therapist and client and that it was wise to be alert to this. Let's return to an examination of the differences between power and control within the therapeutic context, keeping in mind the feminist analysis of power. The distinction between power and control made at the beginning of this chapter allows an explanation of the dynamic between client and therapist within the systemic framework. Perceived control as an issue within the context of client and therapist is understood through reference to the notion of complementarity and symmetricality. Complementary relationships are hierarchically different in that one person is unequal to the other along any one of, or a number of, dimensions, including behaviour, meaning, affect, status or belief. Symmetrical relationships match people along one or many of these dimensions.

There are many factors that contribute towards an unequal (complementary) relationship between therapist and client, not the least of which is exchange of money, the determination of access and the determination of treatment and control of information. The therapist has access to 'expert knowledge' for which the client pays. The client, as seeker of advice, is in a hierarchically inferior position while the therapist, as giver, is in a hierarchically superior position. Haley (1976) argues that the client comes to therapy looking for expert advice. Therefore, the therapist should assume that role. In other words, he argues for an unambiguous relationship between therapist and client. An unambiguous relationship would mean that the therapist would assume responsibility for clarifying the nature of the relationship, the client's expectations, how the 'expert' knowledge will be used and other critical aspects of the complementarity of their beginning relationship.

However, the therapist needs to allow a degree of ambiguity in the client–therapist relationship, increasingly adopting an equal position and using strategies that elicit the client's own resources. In this way, an instability of hierarchical issues in the relationship may result. This instability, expressed in shifting hierarchical positions, may permit an acceptable balance of power as well as coax the client's gradual resumption of control over her own life. At times, I function as teacher, coach, and guide; at other times, change agent, influencer and persuader. At still others, I am confidante, friend and sympathiser. At all times, I am continually learning from my clients, inviting them to be consultants on their own problems. Shifting positions of power and influence seem to be the hallmark of most functional relationships over time: for example, the shifting negotiations about responsibility and control in the parent–adolescent relationship or the myriad shifting roles adopted by flexible marital partners.

Flexibility and adaptability are key factors in any surviving system (Tannen 1991). Any relationship crystallised into either complementary or symmetrical positions would be unresponsive to new information and therefore rigid. Therapy with my clients is a process where the client gradually assumes at least perceived control of her life and where I, as therapist, monitor the processes of the helping relationship and model flexible responses to events in the counselling sessions. Shifting complementary and symmetrical positions need to be incorporated into the client–therapist relationship in order for that relationship to be effective for the client. These shifts facilitate the gradual resumption of sovereignty by the client over her life.

In contrast, symmetrical escalation is a 'tit for tat' matching and then 'one-upping' or increasing the level of control in the interaction between therapist and client. For young women with bulimia nervosa, this process often begins with therapists defining themselves as initiators of change and, therefore (unwittingly), as hostile to the status quo or the stability of the system. Clients recognise the threat and, consciously or unconsciously, protect the familiarity of the status quo.

As much as possible, I try to highlight women's own resources to solve their problems. The main way of doing this is to use questions. If the predominant linguistic form is questioning, then the client will take 'centre stage' as her experiences, goals, perceptions and concerns are repeatedly called forth. Explicitly at least, the therapist takes back stage. If the question is genuinely a question and not a disguised statement, then clients may access their own resources about a problem. Client autonomy is fostered. The client may also feel a sense of personal achievement when problems are overcome in that she has not relied on the 'expert knowledge' of the therapist. 'What would be useful for you to talk about today?'; 'How would you like to approach this topic?'; 'What tasks would you like to try this week?' – these are the kinds of questions that allow the psychological space necessary for client autonomy.

It is perhaps instructive to note that, even with an invitational stance mainly shown through questions, Susanne, Elizabeth and Marie had interpreted the tasks as directives and would consciously undertake them. Although this tendency can be used therapeutically, the therapist needs to encourage self-assertion, as it is this quality that will increase self-awareness and a sense of power in the client to make constructive changes in her life and the society at large.

Specific therapeutic practices which address control

There is a range of successful practices within the systemic tradition that can be increasingly incorporated into the process of therapy, building a greater sense of control in the client over time. Many encourage a symmetrical relationship between client and therapist by stimulating the client to take an 'expert' or 'consultant' role in her own life, for example, inviting the client to be her own therapist, posing dilemmas that encourage choice, admitting therapeutic impotence and providing psychological space for the client to take charge. These and the other practices shown in Table 9.1 that explicitly encourage a symmetric relationship between client and therapist should occur more frequently over time if the client is to resume greater sovereignty.

Table 9.1 Systemic practices that facilitate the clients' sense of perceived control: externalising the problem
Adopting the client's language and perception of the world
Client initiating discussions in session
Suggesting tasks by the client at the end of sessions
Using paradoxical tasks that imply that the client has control of her behaviour
Posing dilemmas that encourage choice
Using language in the dilemmas that bias the shift towards an active role in problems
Using active metaphorical language
Challenging passive self descriptions
Reframing
Highlighting exceptions to problem-saturated self-descriptions
Challenging societal specifications regarding attractiveness
Encouraging a direct connection with emotion and its appropriate expression
Using goal construction questions that elicit the client's resources
Inviting the client to be his/her own therapist
Therapist admitting his/her impotence

The practices cited in Table 9.1 may stimulate clients' sense of perceived choice and should be included in therapeutic procedure. Specific recommendations include:

- the use of paradoxical tasks, such as prescribing a binge, as these are often the first sign of control over a previously uncontrollable problem

- a restraining change task – that is, a 'don't change' prescription that invites the client to observe the pattern of bingeing and vomiting by keeping a record or diary of frequency, events, affect and behaviour

- externalising the problem and relative influence questioning

- the use of goal construction questions early in therapy to define the parameters of therapy and provide indicators for the closure of therapy, otherwise client and therapist may become dependent

- the use of tasks – behavioural and affective – between sessions, which invite the client to please herself and defy the female prescription for pleasing others

- tasks may be stipulated by the therapist early in the treatment phase in order to initiate the change process. However, later in therapy they may be based on client-initiated discussion in the interview. By the end phases of therapy, the client should be invited to be her own therapist and asked to suggest her own tasks.

Control and power: the big picture

How this sense of sovereignty over one's life links back into the client's wider exercise of power is an important issue within the therapeutic domain. It is important to reiterate here that the client's perception of control is different from the notion of power as defined in the opening paragraphs of this chapter. However, the client's perception of control may have implications for her ability to exert power, that is, her ability to effect tangible outcomes in the external world. As stated above, the links between perceptions of control and the wider world of power are recursive and each, depending upon its effect, exacerbates or exaggerates the other. This wider view of therapy may situate therapy more within socio-political spheres rather than as an individual activity. Arguing against the dictates of femininity, advising the defacing of billboards, encouraging self-directed rather than other-directed behaviour has direct implications for the exercise of power in the larger world. The ramifications of such actions need to be examined by therapist and client in the light of the specific context.

Conclusion

It has been my argument throughout this book that the client's growing sense of agency in all four domains is necessary for effective therapy. Traditionally, behavioural and interpersonal themes have been emphasised at the expense of developmental and sociocultural ones. Yet, the role of social and cultural forces is particularly important in developing and maintaining the problem. This was evidenced in the background information on the scope and significance of the problem and also on the themes that emerge during therapy. The analysis of the case studies reinforce these themes. Furthermore the client's sense of lack of control emerged as the central tendency across all domains. It also emerged as the main contender of effectiveness in the therapeutic relationship.

Therapists must recognise this and work with influencing the client, not controlling her. Unless the therapist can model influence without control, the client will not learn new ways of working within her own sphere of activity. There are a number of therapeutic practices that will assist this process that have been suggested in this chapter. The skill in using them depends very much on remaining aware of the processes during therapy. It is the considered application of these practices that should bring effectiveness.

A closing note to the practitioner

There are certainly many ways to use these practices in working with bulimic clients. I have shared my clinical model and the thinking that has gone into its use in the hope that you will find it useful in assisting women with the problem in clinical practice. If you develop more effective techniques that I have not considered, I would like the opportunity to share them with you.

Tests To Be Used In Information Gathering

The measurement of therapeutic efficacy for bulimia nervosa should be gauged from multiple sources, because the problem is itself multi-dimensional. Improvement needs to occur across the four main domains concerning bulimia nervosa – behavioural, interpersonal, developmental and sociocultural. The elimination of bingeing and purging behaviour represents only one part of successful treatment. Success also needs to be measured by progress towards client goals, an increase in less rigid patterns of thinking, improvement in interpersonal relationships (including an increase in the amount of time spent with others), the effective crossing of critical life transitions and involvement in social action. Standardised tests exist that can serve as direct, valid and reliable indices of such progress. In combination, and with due respect for test fatigue, they provide a strong basis for inferring efficacy. They can be used to assess outcomes (pre-, post-test, and long-term follow-up) and, in some instances, process (continuous assessment).

This appendix reviews the existing tests that I have found most relevant for determining both positive and negative change throughout the course of therapy. These are tests for bulimia nervosa, depression, self-esteem, guilt and hostility, body dissatisfaction, body esteem and family environment. (Some of these tests are restricted and will need to be administered, scored and interpreted by registered professionals.)

Tests for bulimia nervosa

The most widely used inventories are the EAT (Garner and Garfinkel 1979), the BULIT-R (Thelen *et al.* 1991) and the Eating Disorder Inventory 2 (EDI–2, Garner 1991).

The EAT is a 40-item self-report inventory presented in 6-point forced choice Likert scale format. Total scores are obtained by giving the most symptomatic response a score of 3, the next most extreme score response a score of 2, and the adjacent less extreme response, a score of 1. No score is given for non-anorexic answers. The EAT was validated using two groups of female anorexic patients (N = 32 and 33) and female controls (N = 34 and 59). Total EAT scores were significantly correlated with criterion group membership (r = 0.87, p<0.001) suggesting a high level of concurrent validity, although there is evidence that, in non-clinical samples, the EAT has been found to have a high false-positive rate for capturing anorexia. High EAT scorers in non-clinical samples have been found to include a range of non-anorexic individuals such as bulimics, sub-clinical anorexics, purgers and obsessional dieters.

The BULIT-R is a 36-item self-report inventory differentiating bulimic women from all other women, including women who do not have an eating disorder and those with other eating disorders and eating disordered behaviour. All 36 items are presented in a 5-point Likert scale format (1 point is given for extreme 'normal' responses and 5 points for extreme 'bulimic' responses). Total scores are obtained by summing across only 28 of the items. Total scores can range from 28 to 140, and 104 is the cut-off for classification as bulimic. The BULIT-R is highly predictive of a DSM-IV diagnosis of bulimia, as indicated by clinical interviews and clinician judgements.

The EDI–2 contains 91 questions loading on eight sub-scales and three provisional sub-scales. These are: drive for thinness, bulimia, body dissatisfaction, ineffectiveness, perfectionism, interpersonal distrust, interoceptive awareness and maturity fears. Subjects rate whether each item applies 'always', 'usually', 'often', 'sometimes', 'rarely' or 'never'. The most extreme anorexic responses, 'always' or 'never' depending on the keyed direction, are scored 3 and adjacent responses 2 and 1 respectively. Sub-scale scores are then computed by summing scores on items in each sub-scale. Elevated scores on two sub-scales in particular (drive for thinness and bulimia) indicate a high likelihood of engaging in eating disordered behaviours (Garner 1991). Internal and test-retest reliability measures for the sub-scales of the EDI–2 for bulimics ranged quite high, from 0.85 to 0.90, and for college samples ranged from 0.65 to 0.93 (Garner 1991).

Tests for depression

The revised Beck Depression Inventory (BDI) (Beck 1987) is a 21-item self-report 4-scale measurement of the severity of depressive symptoms (Beck and Steer 1993). Respondents endorse no complaint (0) to a severe complaint (3) to indicate how they have been feeling in the past week. Previous research has established the BDI to be a valid and reliable measure of depression. The inventory has also been correlated with other respected tests of depression. The BDI has been used many times as a measure of depression in bulimic samples.

The Reynolds Adolescent Depression Scale is designed to assess depression in adolescents aged 13 to 18 years (Reynolds 1987). It consists of 30 items and uses a 4-point Likert-type scale response format ('almost never', 'hardly ever', 'sometimes' or 'most of the time'). The higher the total RAD score, the greater the level of depressive symptomatology. The validity and reliability of this test is supported by moderate to high test–retest reliabilities, strong internal consistency and strong criterion correlations with other respected adolescent depression tests.

Tests for self-esteem

The Coopersmith Self-esteem Inventory (1981) measures evaluative attitudes towards the self in social, work, family and personal areas of experience. The adult form, designed for persons 16 years of age and above, consists of 25 short statements and subjects are asked to respond with either 'like me' or 'unlike me'. A total score on the SEI has been found to have internal coefficients ranging from 0.71 to 0.92, split half reliability coefficients ranging from 0.87 to 0.90, and test–retest reliability coefficients of 0.88 (5 weeks) and 0.70 (3 years). The measure has been found to correlate with other measures of known reliability and validity.

Tests for guilt and hostility

The Buss-Durkee Inventory (B-DI) is a clinical scale for the self-assessment of anger and guilt (Buss and Durkee 1957). The original B-DI had eight sub-scales including assault, overt hostility, covert hostility and suspicion.

Tests for body dissatisfaction

One method for measuring body dissatisfaction is a silhouette technique in which a range of body size drawings are presented to subjects (Stunkard, Sorenson and Schulsinger 1980). These range from very thin (1) to very obese (9). Subjects are asked to rate which drawings best match their current figure and their ideal figure. Perceptual body dissatisfaction is calculated by subtracting the ideal from the current figure yielding a discrepancy score. The technique appears to have good test–retest reliability and adequate validity.

Body esteem is measured using the Body Esteem Scale (Franzoi and Shields 1984). Subjects are asked to rate how they feel about themselves regarding 35 different body parts and functions. Each item is rated on a 5-point Likert scale (from 1 = strong negative feelings to 5 = strong positive feelings). The scale contains three sub-scales: sexual attractiveness, weight concern and physical condition. Scores on the BES correlate with measures of self-esteem.

Tests for perception of family environment

The Family Environment Scale – Real Form (FES; Moos and Moos 1986) is a 90-item inventory designed to assess perceptions of family climate. It consists of ten sub-scales including cohesion, conflict and control. Each sub-scale contains nine brief statements for which respondents must indicate true or false, depending on how descriptive the statements are for their family. Validity and reliability is attested to by high internal consistency, high test–retest coefficients and strong correlations with other valid test measures of family functioning.

References

Abraham, S., Mira, M., Beumont, P., Sowerbutts, T. and Llewellyn-Jones, D. (1983) 'Eating behaviours among young women.' *Medical Journal of Australia 2*, 225–228.

Allen, F.C., Scannel, E.D. and Turner, H.R. (1998) 'Guilt and hostility as coexisting characteristics of Bulimia Nervosa.' *Australian Psychologist 33*, 2, 143–147.

American Psychiatric Association (1994) *Diagnostic and Statistical Manual of Mental Disorders fourth edition.* Washington, DC: The American Psychiatric Association.

Andensen, H. and Goolishian, H. (1988) 'Humans systems as linguistic systems: Preliminary and evolving ideas about the implications for clinical theory.' *Family Process 27*, 371–394.

Arkes, H. R. (1991) 'Costs and benefits of judgment errors. Implications for debiasing.' *Psychological Bulletin 110*, 3, 486–498.

Arnow, B. (1999) 'Introduction.' *Journal of Clinical Psychology 55*, 6, 669–674.

Attie, I. and Brooks-Gunn, J. (1992) 'Developmental issues in the study of eating problems and disorders.' In J. H. Crowther, P. L. Tannenbaum, S. E. Hobfoll, and M. A. P. Stephens (eds) *The Etiology of Bulimia Nervosa: The Individual and Familial Context.* Washington DC: Hemisphere Publishing Corporation.

Ball, K., Kenardy, J. and Lee, C. (1999) 'Relationships between disordered eating and unwanted sexual experiences: A review.' *Australian Psychologist 34*, 3, 166–176.

Barr-Taylor, C., Sharpe, T., Shisslak, C., Bryson, S., Estes, L., Gray, N., McKnight, K., Crago, M., Kraemer, H. and Killen, J. (1998) 'Shame.' *International Journal of Eating Disorders 24*, 1, 31–42.

Bateson, G. (1979a) *Steps to an Ecology of Mind.* New York: Chandler Publishing Company.

Bateson, G. (1979b) *Mind and Nature: A Necessary Unity.* New York: E. P. Dutton.

Beck, A.T. (1987) *Beck Depression Inventory.* San Antonio: Harcourt Brace.

Beck, A. T. and Steer, R. A. (1993) *Beck Depression Inventory Manual.* San Antonio: Psychological Corporation.

Berger, J. (1972) *Ways of Seeing.* Harmondsworth: Penguin.

Bhadrinath, B. R. (1990) 'Anorexia nervosa in adolescents of Asian extraction.' *British Journal of Psychiatry 156*, 565–568.

Blinder, B. and Chao, K. (1994) 'Eating disorders: A historical perspective.' In L. Alexander-Mott and D. Lumsden (eds) *Understanding Eating Disorders: Anorexia Nervosa, Bulimia Nervosa and Obesity.* Washington DC: Taylor and Francis.

Boscolo, L. (1991) *Unpublished workshop notes.* Sydney, Australia.

Boscolo, L., Bertrando, P., Fiocco, P. M., Palvarini, R. M. and Pereira, J. (1994) 'Language and change: The use of keywords in therapy.' *The Australian and New Zealand Journal of Family Therapy 16,* 2, 57–63.

Braun, D., Sunday, S., Huang, A. and Halmi, K. (1999) 'More males seek treatment for eating disorders.' *International Journal of Eating Disorders 25,* 4, 415–424.

Brouwers, M. (1990) 'Treatment of body image dissatisfaction with women with Bulimia Nervosa.' *Journal of Counseling and Development 69,* 2, 144–147.

Brown, J.E. (1994) 'Teaching hypothesizing skills from a post-Milan perspective.' *The Australian and New Zealand Journal of Family Therapy 16,* 3, 133–142.

Brown, J. E. (1997) 'Circular questioning: An introductory guide.' *Australian and New Zealand Journal of Family Therapy 18,* 2, 109–114.

Brown, J. E. (1999) 'Bowen family systems theory and practice: Illustration and critiques.' *The Australian and New Zealand Journal of Family Therapy 20,* 2, 94–103.

Brownmiller, S. (1986) *Femininity.* London: Paladin Grafton Books.

Bruch, H. (1973) *Eating Disorders: Obesity, Anorexia and the Person Within.* New York: Basic Books.

Bruch, H. (1978) *The Golden Cage: The Enigma of Anorexia Nervosa.* London: Open Books.

Bugental, J. (1990) *Intimate Journeys: Stories from Life-changing Therapy.* San Francisco: Jossey-Bass.

Buss, A. H., and Durkee, A. (1957) 'An inventory for assessing different kinds of hostility.' *Journal of Consulting Psychology 21,* 4, 343–349.

Button, E. J. and Whitehouse, A. (1981) 'Subclinical anorexia nervosa.' *Psychological Medicine 11,* 509–516.

Carlat, D. J. and Camargo, C. A. (1991) 'Review of bulimia nervosa in males.' *American Journal of Psychiatry 148,* 831–843.

Clarke, M. G. and Palmer, R. L. (1983) 'Eating attitudes and neurotic symptoms in university students.' *British Journal of Psychiatry 142,* 299–304.

Connell R. W. (1987) *Gender and Power: Society, the Person and Sexual Politics.* Sydney: Allen and Unwin.

Connors, M. E. and Morse, N. (1993) 'Sexual abuse and eating disorders: A review.' *International Journal of Eating Disorders 13,* 1, 1–12.

Coopersmith, S. (1981) *Self-Esteem Inventories.* Paulo Alto, CA: Consulting Psychologists Press.

Crowther, J. H., Wolf, E. M. and Sherwood, N. E. (1992) 'Epidemiology of bulimia nervosa.' In J. H. Crowther, P. L. Tannenbaum, S. E. Hobfoll, and M. A. P. Stephens (eds) *The Etiology of Bulimia Nervosa: The Individual and Familial Context.* Washington DC: Hemisphere Publishing Corporation.

Davis, C. and Katzman, M. (1999) 'Perfection as acculturation: Psychological correlates of eating problems in Chinese male and female students living in the United States.' *International Journal of Eating Disorders 25*, 1, 65–70.

Davis, C. and Yager, J. (1992) 'Transcultural aspects of eating disorders: A critical literature review.' *Cultural Medical Psychiatry 16*, 3, 377–394.

de Shazer, S. (1982) *Patterns of Brief Family Therapy.* New York: The Guilford Press.

de Shazer, S. (1985) *Keys to Solution in Brief Therapy.* New York: W.W. Norton.

Duker, M. and Slade, R. (1988) *Anorexia Nervosa and Bulimia: How to Help.* Pennsylvania: Open University Press.

Dwyer, J. T., Feldman, J. J., Seltzer, C. C. and Mayer, J. (1969) 'Adolescent attitudes towards weight and appearance.' *Journal of Nutrition Education 1*, 14–19.

Epston, D. and Madigan, S. (1995) 'Therapeutic intervention: The cause or the cure.' *The Undead: The Magazine of the Vancouver Anti-Anorexia Anti-Bulimia League 1*, 1, 8–11.

Evans, J. (1989) *Bias in Hunman Reasoning: Causes and Consequnences.* Hove and London: Lawrence Erlbaum and Associates.

Fairburn, C. G. and Beglin, S. J. (1990) 'Studies of the epidemiology of bulimia nervosa.' *American Journal of Psychiatry 147*, 401–408.

Flaskas, C. (1990) 'Power and Knowledge: the Care of the new epistemology. *Australian and New Zealand Journal of Family Therapy 11*, 207–214.

Foucault, M. (1984) *Power and Knowledge: Selected Interviews and Other Writings.* New York: Pantheon.

Franzoi, S. L. and Shields, S. A. (1984) 'The Body Esteem Scale: Multidimensional structure and sex differences in a college population.' *Journal of Personality Assessment 48*, 2, 173–178.

Fredrickson, B. L. and Roberts, T. (1997) 'Objectification theory: Towards understanding women's lived experience and mental health risks.' *Psychology of Women Quarterly 21*, 173–206.

Fredrickson, B. L., Noll, S., Roberts, T., Quinn, D. and Twenge, J. M. (1998) 'That swimsuit becomes you: Sex differences in self-objectification, restrained eating and math performance.' *Journal of Personality and Social Psychology 75*, 1, 269–284.

Furlong, M. and Lipp, J. (1994) 'The multiple relationships between neutrality and therapeutic influence.' *The Australian and New Zealand Journal of Family Therapy 16*, 3, 113–122.

Furnham, A. and Patel, R. (1994) 'The eating attitudes and behaviors of Asian and British school girls: A pilot study.' *The International Journal of Social Psychology 40*, 214–226.

Garner, D. M. (1991) *EDI–2: Eating Disorder Inventory – 2 Professional Manual.* Odessa, FL.: Psychological Assessment Resources.

Garner, D. M. and Garfinkel, P. E. (1979) 'The eating attitudes test: An index of the symptoms of anorexia nervosa.' *Psychological Medicine 9*, 273–279.

Gleaves, D. H., Williamson. D. H. and Barker, S. E. (1993) 'Confirmatory factor analysis of a multidimensional model of bulimia nervosa.' *Journal of Abnormal Psychology 102*, 1, 173–176.

Goode, E. (1985) 'Medical aspects of the Bulimic Syndrome and Bulimarexia.' *Transactional Analysis Journal 15*, 1 January.

Green, D. W. (1990) 'Confirmation bias, problem solving and cognitive models. In J. Caverni, J. Fabre and M. Gonzales (eds) *Cognitive Bias*. Amsterdam: Elsevier Science Publishers.

Grigg, D., Friesen, J. D. and Sheppy, M. I. (1989) 'Family patterns associated with anorexia nervosa.' *Journal of Marital and Family Therapy 15*, 29–42.

Haley, J. (1976) *Problem Solving Therapy*. New York: Harper and Row.

Hall, A. and Hay, P. (1991) 'Eating disorder patient referrals from a population region 1977–1986.' *Psychological Medicine 21*, 697–701.

Hamilton, A. (1999) 'The effects of psychotherapy on persons with bulimia nervosa.' *Unpublished doctoral thesis*. The Australian National University.

Hamilton, M., Meade, C. and Gelwick, B. (1980) 'Incidence and severity of eating disorders on two campuses.' *Paper presented at the 88th annual convention of the American Psychological Association* (1979) *Montreal*.

Hart, K. E. and Chiovari, P. (1998) 'Inhibition of eating behavior: Negative cognitive effects of dieting.' *Journal of Clinical Psychology 54*, 4, 427–430.

Hatsukami, D., Mitchell, J.E., Eckert, E. and Pyle, R. P. (1986) 'Characteristics of patients with bulimia only, bulimia with affective disorder, and bulimia with substance abuse problems.' *Addictive Behavior 11*, 399–406.

Hawkins, R., Fremouw, W. and Clement, P. (1984) (eds) *The Binge-Purge Syndrome*. New York: Springer Publishing Company.

Haynes, S., Huland-Spain, S. and Oliviera, J. (1993) 'Identifying causal relationships in clinical assessment.' *Psychological Assessment 5*, 3, 281–291.

Heatherton, T. F., Todd, F., Nichols, P., Mahemedi, F. and Keel, P. (1995) 'Body weight, dieting, and eating disorder symptoms among college students 1982 to 1992.' *American Journal of Psychiatry 152*, 11, 1623–1629.

Herman, K.C. (1993) 'Reassuring predictors of therapist competence.' *Journal of Counseling and Development 72*, 29–32.

Hirt, E. R. and Markman, K. D. (1995) 'Multiple explanation: A consider-an-alternative strategy for debiasing judgments.' *Journal of Personality and Social Psychology 60*, 1069–1086.

Hoek, H.W. (1993) 'Review of the epidemiological studies of eating disorders.' *International Review of Psychiatry 5*, 61–74.

Huon, G.F. (1994) 'Dieting, binge eating and some of their correlates among secondary schoolgirls.' *International Journal of Eating Disorders 15*, 2, 159–164.

Kaplan, A.S., Garfinkel, P.E. and Brown, G.M. (1989) 'The DST and TRH test in bulimia nervosa.' *British Journal of Psychiatry 154*, 86–92.

Kayrooz, C. (1991) *A Systematic Cybernetic Couselling Approach with Women who have Bulimia Nervosa*. Unpublished Masters manuscript. University of Canberra.

Keel P. K. and Mitchell, J. E. (1997) 'Outcome in bulimia nervosa.' *American Journal of Psychiatry 154*, 313–321.

Keel P. K. and Mitchell J. E. (1999) 'Mortality from eating disorders – A 5 to 10 year record linkage study.' *International Journal of Eating Disorders 26*, 97–101.

Keel P. K., Mitchell, J. E., Miller, K., Davis, T. and Crow, S. (2000) 'Social adjustment over 10 years following diagnosis with bulimia nervosa.' *International Journal of Eating Disorders 27*, 1, 21–28.

Kendler, K. S., MacLean, C., Neale, M., Kessler, H., Heath, A. and Eaves, L. (1991) 'The genetic epidemiology of bulimia nervosa.' *American Journal of Psychiatry 148*, 1627–1637.

Kenny, D. and Adams, R. (1994) 'The relationship between eating attitudes, body mass index, age, and gender in Australian university students.' *Australian Psychologist 29*, 128–134.

Keren, G. (1990) 'Cognitive aids and debiasing methods: Can cognitive pills cure cognitive ills?' In J. Caverni, J. Fabre and M. Gonzales (eds) *Cognitive Bias*. North Holland: Elsevier Science Publishers.

King, M. B. (1989) 'Eating disorders in general practice.' *British Medical Journal 293*, 1412–1414.

Klerman, G. L., Weissman, M. N., Rounsaville, B. J. and Chevron, E. S. (1984) *Interpersonal Psychotherapy of Depression*. New York: Basic Books.

Klesges, R., Mizes, J. and Klesges, L. (1987) 'Self-help dieting strategies in college males and females.' *International Journal of Eating Disorders 6*, 409–417.

Kraner, M. and Ingram, M. (1997) 'Busting out – breaking free. A group program for young women wanting to reclaim their lives from anorexia nervosa.' *Gecko 3*, 31–54.

Lacey, J. H. (1990) 'Incest, incestuous fantasy and indecency: A clinical catchment area study of normal weight bulimic women.' *British Journal of Psychiatry 157*, 399–403.

Lacey, J. and Birtchnell, S. (1985) 'Binge-eating and the bulimic syndrome.' *Update* March, 43–51.

Langer, E. (1983) *The Psychology of Control*. Beverly Hills: Sage Publications.

Lenoux, P., Steiger, H. and Jabalpurlawa, S. (2000) 'State/trait distinctions in bulimic syndromes.' *International Journal of Eating Disorders 27*, 36–42.

Lerner, S. and Lerner, H. (1983) 'A systems approach to resistance: Theoretical and technical considerations.' *American Journal of Psychotherapy 37*, 387–399.

Levey, J., McDermott, S. and Lee, C. (1989) 'Current issues in Bulimia Nervosa.' *Australian Psychologist 24*, 2, 171–185.

Littlewood, R. (1995) 'Psychopathology and personal agency: Modernity, culture change and eating disorders in South Asian societies.' *British Journal of Medical Psychology 68*, 45–63.

Lobsinger, C. (1997) 'Addiction power and gender.' *The Australian and New Zealand Journal of Family Therapy 18*, 4, 210–215.

Logue, A. W. (1991) *The Psychology of Eating and Drinking* second edition. New York: W. H. Freeman.

Lohyn, M. (1994) 'Naomi Wolf and the new feminism.' *The Australian and New Zealand Journal of Family Therapy 15*, 3, 143–149.

Luepnitz, D. (1988) *The Family Interpreted*. New York: Basic Books.

Madanes, C. (1981) *Strategic Family Therapy*. Los Angeles: Jossey-Bass.

Madigan, S. (1994) 'Body politics.' *Networker* November/December 27.

Martin, M. C. and Gentry, J. W. (1997) 'Stuck in the model trap: the effects of beautiful models in ads on female pre-adolescents and adolescents.' *The Journal of Advertising 26*, 2, 19–33.

McCarthy, M. (1990) 'The thin ideal, depression and eating disorders in women.' *Behavioral Research and Therapy 28*, 205–215.

McFarland, B. (1997) 'Food angst: Swords into plowshares.' *Networker* May/June, 37–43.

McGregor, H. (1990) 'Conceptualising male violence against female partners.' *The Australian and New Zealand Journal of Family Therapy 11*, 2, 65–70.

McLennan, J., Twigg K. and Bezant, B. (1993) 'Therapist construct systems in use during psychotherapy interviews.' *Journal of Clinical Psychology 49*, 543–550.

Miller, D. A. F. (1993) 'The relationship between childhood sexual abuse and subsequent onset of bulimia nervosa.' *Child Abuse and Neglect: The International Journal 17*, 2, 305–314.

Minuchin, S. (1974) *Families and Family Therapy*. London: Tavistock Publications.

Mislkind, M., Rodin, J., Silberstein, L. R. and Striegal-Moore, R. H. (1986) 'The embodiment of masculinity: Cultural, psychological and behavioural dimensions.' *American Behavioral Scientist 29*, 545–562.

Moley, V. (1983) 'Interactional treatment of eating disorders.' *Journal of Strategic Therapies 2*, 4, 7–9.

Monteath, S.A. and McCabe, M.P. (1997) 'The influence of societal factors on female body image.' *The Journal of Social Psychology 137*, 6, 708–727.

Moos, R.H. and Moos, B.S. (1986) *Family Environment Scale Manual*. Palo Alto, CA: Consulting Psychologists.

Murphy, M. (1997) *Drop a Dress Size by the Weekend...Yeah, Sure!* Victoria: Body Image and Better Health Program.

Nasser, M. (1988) 'Culture and weight consciousness of psychosomatic research.' *Journal of Psychosomatic Research 32*, 6, 573–577.

Nasser, M. (1997) Culture and Weight Consciousness. New York: Routledge.

Nevo, S. (1985) 'Bulimic symptoms: Prevalence and ethnic differences among college women.' *International Journal of Eating Disorders 4*, 2, 151–168.

Nezu, A. M. and Nezu, C. M. (1993) 'Identifying and selecting target problems for clinical intervention: A problem solving model.' *Psychological Assessment 5*, 3, 254–263.

Nylund, D. and Thomas, J. (1994) 'The economics of narrative.' *Networker* November/December 38–39.

O'Connor, J. (1984) 'Strategic individual psychotherapy with bulimic women.' *Psychotherapy 21*, 491–499.

Orbach, S. (1978) *Fat is a Feminist Issue*. New York: Paddington Press.

Orbach, S. (1986) *Hunger Strike. The Anorectic's Struggle as a Metaphor in Our Age.* New York: W.W. Norton and Company.

Patton, G. C., Johnson-Sabine, E., Wood, K., Mann, A.H., and Wakeling, A.W. (1990) 'Abnormal eating attitudes in London school girls. A prospective epidemiological study: Outcome at twelve months.' *Psychological Medicine 20*, 383–394.

Polivy, J. and Herman, C. (1985) 'Dieting and bingeing. A causal analysis.' *American Psychologist 40*, 2, 193–201.

Pope, H., Jonas, J., Hudson, J. and Yurgelun-Tod, D. (1983) 'Family history study of anorexia and bulimia.' *British Journal of Psychiatry 142*, 133–138.

Pyle, R., Mitchell, J. and Eckert, E. (1981) 'Bulimia: A report of 34 cases.' *Journal of Clinical Psychiatry 42*, 60–64.

Reynolds, W. M. (1987) *Reynolds Adolescent Depression Scale: Professional Manual.* Odessa, FL: Psychological Assessment Resources.

Root, M. P. (1991) 'Persistent, disordered eating as a gender-specific, post-traumatic stress response to sexual assault.' *Psychotherapy 28*, 96–102.

Root, M. P., Fallon, P. and Friedrich, W. (1986) *Bulimia: A Systems Approach to Treatment.* New York: W. W. Norton.

Rosen, J. and Gross, J. (1989) 'Prevalence of weight reducing and weight gaining in adolescent girls and boys.' *Health Psychology 6*, 131–147.

Russell, G.F. (1979) 'Bulimia nervosa: An ominous varient of anorexia nervosa.' *Psychological Medicine 9*, 429–448.

Ryan, B. and Roughan, P. (1984) 'Women and weight: A treatment programme for both normal and overweight women preoccupied by eating and related issues.' *Australian Journal of Family Therapy 5*, 4, 267–274.

Schur, E., Sanders, M. and Steiner, H. (2000) 'Body dissatisfaction and dieting in young children.' *International Journal of Eating Disorders 27*, 1, 74–82.

Selvini-Palazzoli, M., Boscolo, L., Cecchin, G.F. and Prata, G. (1974) 'The treatment of children through the brief therapy of their parents.' *Family Process 13*, 429–442.

Selvini-Palazzoli, M., Boscolo, L., Cecchin, G. and Prata, G. (1978) *Paradox and Counter Paradox.* New York: Jason Aronson.

Shapero, D. A. and Shapero, D. (1982) 'Meta-analysis of comparative therapy outcome studies: A replication and refinement.' *Psychological Bulletin 92*, 581–604.

Shifren K., Furnham A. and Bauserman R. L. (1998) 'Instrumental and expressive eating traits: A replication across American and British students.' *Personality and Individual Differences 25*, 1–17.

Smith, M. L. and Glass, G. V. (1977) 'Meta-analysis of psychotherapy outcome studies.' *American Psychologist 32*, 753–760.

Spangler, D. L. (1999) 'Cognitive-behavioural therapy for bulimia nervosa: An illustration.' *Journal of Clinical Psychology 4*, 2, 699–713.

Stein, D.M. (1991) 'The prevalence of bulimia: A review of the empirical research.' *Journal of Nutrition Education 23*, 5, 205–213.

Stevens, C. and Tiggemann, M. (1998) 'Women's body figure preferences across the lifespan.' *Journal of Genetic Psychology 159*, 1, 94–102.

Stice, E. and Shaw, H. E. (1994) 'Adverse effects of the media portrayed thin-ideal on women and linkages to bulimic symptomatology.' *Journal of Social and Clinical Psychology 13*, 3, 288–308.

Stice, E. (1999) 'Clinical implications of psychosocial research on bulimia nervosa and binge-eating disorder.' *Journal of Clinical Psychology 54*, 4, 675–683.

Striegal-Moore, R. H. (1992) 'Prevention of bulimia nervosa.' In J. H. Crowther, P. L. Tannenbaum, S. E. Hobfoll, and M. A. P. Stephens *The Etiology of Bulimia Nervosa: The Individual and Familial Context.* Washington DC: Hemisphere Publishing Corporation.

Stunkard, A.J. (1959) 'Eating patterns of obese persons.' Psychiatric Quarterly 33, 284–292.

Stunkard, A. J., Sorenson, T. and Schulsinger, F. (1980) 'Use of the Danish Adoption Register for the study of obesity and thinness.' In S. Kety (ed) *The Genetics of Neurological and Psychiatric Disorders.* New York: Raven Press.

Szmukler, G. I. (1983) 'Weight and food preoccupation in a population of English schoolgirls.' In J. G. Bergman (ed) *Understanding Anorexia Nervosa and Bulimia: Fourth Ross Conference on Medical Research.* Columbus, OH: Ross Laboratories.

Tannen, D. (1991) *You Just Don't Understand.* Australia: Random House.

Thelen, M. H., Farmer, J., Wonderlich, S. and Smith, M. (1991) 'A revision of the Bulimia Test: The BULIT-R.' *Psychological Assessment: A Journal of Consulting and Clinical Psychology 3*, 119–124.

Tiggeman, M. and Pickering, A. (1996) 'Role of television in adolescent women's body dissatisfaction and drive for thinness.' *International Journal of Eating Disorders 20*, 2, 199–203.

Tiggeman, M. and Rothblum, E. (1988) 'Gender differences in social consequences of perceived overweight in the United States and Australia.' *Sex Roles 18*, 1/2, 75–86.

Touyz, S. (1984) 'Bulimia: Food for thought.' *Modern Medicine of Australia* Oct. 40–50.

Touyz, S. and Beumont, P. (1985) (eds) *Eating Disorders. Prevalence and Treatment.* Sydney: Williams and Wilkins.

Toynbee, A. (1972) *A Study of History.* London: Oxford University Press.

Turnell, A. and Lipchik, E. (1999) 'The role of empathy in brief therapy.' *The Australian and New Zealand Journal of Family Therapy 20*, 4, 177–182.

Vognsen, J. (1985) 'Individual therapy. Brief strategic treatment of Bulimia.' *Transactional Analysis Journal 15*, 1, 79–84.

Waller, G. (1992) 'Sexual abuse and the severity of bulimic symptoms.' *British Journal of Psychiatry 161*, 90–93.

Watts, W. and Ellis, A. (1992) 'Drug abuse and eating disorders: Prevention implications.' *Journal of Drug Education 22*, 223–240.

Watzlawick, P., Weakland, J.H. and Fisch, R. (1974) *Change: Principles of Problem Formation and Problem Resolution.* New York: W.W. Norton.

Weakland, J. (1990) *Unpublished workshop notes.* Sydney, Australia.

Weiss, L., Katzman, M. and Wolchik, S. (1994) 'Bulimia Nervosa: Definition, diagnostic criteria, and associated psychological problems.' In L. Alexander-Mott and D. Lumsden (eds) *Understanding Eating Disorders: Anorexia Nervosa, Bulimia Nervosa and Obesity*. Washington DC: Taylor and Francis.

Welch, S. L. and Fairburn, C. (1996) 'Childhood sexual and physical abuse as risk factors for the development of bulimia nervosa: A community based case control study.' *Child Abuse and Neglect: The International Journal 20*, 7, 633–642.

Whitaker A., Davies, M., Shaffer, D., Johnson, J., Abrams, S., Walsh, B. T. and Kalikow, K. (1989) 'The struggle to be thin: A survey of anorexic and bulimic symptoms in a non-referred adolescent population.' *Psychological Medicine 19*, 143–163.

White, M. (1986a) *Anorexia Nervosa: A Cybernetic Perspective. Selected Papers*. Adelaide: Dulwich Centre Publications.

White, M. (1989) 'The externalizing of the problem.' Dulwich Centre Newsletter, Summer.

White, M. (1990) *Notes from an Intensive Training Session*. Adelaide: South Australia.

White, M. (1991) Unpublished notes from a workshop. Canberra ACT.

White, M. and Epston, D. (1989) *Literate Means to Therapeutic Ends*. Adelaide: Dulwich Centre Publications.

Wilson, G.T. 'Toward the understanding and treatment of binge eating.' In Hawkins, R., Fremouw, W. and Clement, P. (1984) (eds) *The Binge-Purge Syndrome*. New York: Springer Publishing Company.

Wilson, G. T. and Fairburn, C. (1998) 'Treatments for eating disorders.' In P. E. Nathan and J. M. Gorman (eds) *A Guide to Treatments that Work*. New York: Oxford University Press.

Wolf, N. (1990) *The Beauty Myth*. London: Vintage.

Wolf, N. (1993) *Fire with Fire: The New Female Power and How it will Change in the 21st Century*. London: Chatto and Windus.

Wonderlich S. (1992) 'Relationship of family and personality factors in bulimia.' In J. H. Crowther, P. L. Tannenbaum, S. E. Hobfoll and M. A. P. Stephens (eds) *The Etiology of Bulimia Nervosa: The Individual and Familial Context. Washington DC: Hemisphere Publishing Corporation*.

Woodman, M. and Dickson, E. (1996) *Dancing in the Flames: The Dark Goddess and the New Mythology*. St Leonards, NSW: Allen and Unwin.

Ziolko, H. U. (1996) 'Bulimia: A historical outline.' *International Journal of Eating Disorders 20*, 4, 345–358.

Subject Index

Author Index

Printed in the United Kingdom
by Lightning Source UK Ltd.
122122UK00001B/130-144/A